MW00413099

RAISING CHAMPION CHILDREN FOR GOD

How to Build Faith and Character into Your Children

by
Billy Joe Daugherty

Raising Champion Children for God
(How to Build Faith and Character
into Your Children)
ISBN 978-1-56267-665-0
Copyright © 2009 by
Billy Joe Daugherty
Victory Christian Center
7700 South Lewis Avenue
Tulsa, Oklahoma 74136-7700 U.S.A.
Web site: www.victory.com

Text Design: Lisa Simpson www.simpsonproductions.net

CONTENTS

INTRODUCTION

Having raised four children who are now grown, Sharon and I know firsthand the joys of parenting, and also what it means to be in the trenches doing warfare on behalf of our kids, even now that they're adults. Here are five great truths to remember. First, God has given the parents the assignment to raise godly children. Second, He is always faithful to His promises. Third, the power of the Holy Spirit is available to us. Fourth, God has given us biblical tools and principles to guide us. And fifth, regardless of our situations, whether our kids are three or twenty-three, we *can* absolutely raise champions for Him! Our four kids have gone through their own struggles, but they're overcoming in their lives and are living all-out for the Lord. They're champions for God. None of us are perfect but we can be overcoming daily.

A champion for God is someone who is an overcomer for God, living according to His standards and pursuing Him. Raising champions for God is what this book is all about. It's designed to equip and encourage you to do more than merely raise your children, but to advance God's Kingdom through them. This is not just any kind of parenting book, but a book for parents who would dare to believe for God's best concerning their children and then are willing to act on that belief.

The tools and principles contained in the following pages come directly from God's Word and from Sharon and my many years of parenting coupled together with almost three decades of being pastors of Victory Christian Center and leaders of Victory Christian School. Being in these positions has allowed us a unique perspective in which to encourage you. Time and time again we've seen God come through mightily in our own family and in the families of others. We've messed up at times and we too need to work on the issues that are presented in the following pages.

The personal stories tell of our mistakes and successes and are to encourage. Sharon and I felt led of God to write this book to share information that would inspire all of us parents to go higher and stronger in our parenting. Sharon and I both know beyond a shadow of a doubt that what is set forth in this book works. It's tried and true. Our goal is that you would not feel condemnation, but after reading this book you would pray, "Lord, show me the adjustments and positive changes that I need to make those changes in order to be a more effective parent. Please help me, Lord, to make them and to learn even more."

My sincere prayer for you as you read on is that you would be encouraged, equipped, and built up in your faith so you can go out and raise champions for God who will impact the world!

Billy Joe Daugherty

1

A HIGH CALLING

"Do not provoke your children to wrath, but bring them up in the training and admonition of the Lord."

— *Ephesians 6:4*

Being a Mom or Dad is a high calling in the Kingdom of God, it's a holy assignment, a divine mission, and an awesome responsibility, a calling on which the future of the whole world pivots. You see, from the beginning of time, God has set the family as His supreme institution for the foundation of society and of the Church. The family is also God's chosen instrument for the execution of His plan throughout history and in these last days.

Children Are a Heritage from the Lord

Psalm 127:3-5 says, *"Behold, children are a **heritage** from the Lord, the fruit of the womb is a reward.*

*Like **arrows** in the hand of a warrior, so are the children of one's youth. Happy is the man who has his quiver full of them; they shall not be ashamed, but shall speak with their enemies in the **gate**."*

This is probably one of the most well-known passages of scripture in regard to the joys of having children, but what does it actually mean? To start with, a *heritage* is much more than just having great family times around the kitchen table and someone to care for you when you're old. It's more than reunions and family photos. A heritage is a godly legacy, a spiritual tradition based on principles for living that are passed on to generations after you are gone. The truths of scripture that we pour into our kids, the training and admonition in the Lord that we give them, are not just so they can be protected and experience the wonders of a relationship with God. As important as those are, raising godly children is also so they can in turn pour what's inside of them out and into those in their own circles of influence. It's so they can carry on the message of the Kingdom and impact the world for God.

The Purpose of the High Calling
as a Parent

Why does the Psalmist compare our children to *arrows* for a warrior? Well, what does a warrior do with arrows? He shoots them against the enemy. One of the main purposes for raising champions for God is to destroy the works of the enemy. Children advance the Kingdom of God. The *gate* in the above passage represents a place of authority and influence in the city. When we invest in the godly training of our kids, God's Word declares that in due time they will unashamedly proclaim His message to a lost and dying world. Also, they will be promoted to places of authority and confront the enemy. They are like sharp arrows. God desires that our children be champions who will pierce the world with godliness and excellence in every arena of society.

It all started back in Genesis, chapter 1. God's plan for Adam and Eve was that they *"multiply and replenish the earth."* Why was it important to fill the earth? What was God after? He was after a godly seed. God wanted children, lots of children who would love Him, serve Him, and honor Him—children who would have dominion, replenish, subdue, and take charge of the earth. You might say, "God loves big families!" He desires to have a rule of righteousness, love, and peace upon this earth and it will only occur through the raising up of godly seed. Why do you think the enemy comes so heavily against the family? It's because he knows that if he can tear apart the family and corrupt the family's seed, then he can destroy a society and thwart whole generations.

The Agenda Against the Family

Homosexual rights advocates, savvy politicians pushing ungodly agendas, humanists with atheistic and evolutionary values, and communists, all know the way to change a nation is to get to its kids. So that's who they target. The communist leader and author Cleon Skousen said point blank the goal of communism (and you can insert any of the above agendas) is to . . .

> ❧
>
> THE GOAL OF COMMUNISM IS TO GET CONTROL OF THE SCHOOLS.
>
> ❧

Get control of the schools.
Use them as transmission belts for socialism.
Break down cultural standards of morality and

present homosexuality, degeneracy, and promiscuity as "normal, natural, and healthy." Discredit the family as an institution and encourage easy divorce. Emphasize the need to raise children away from the negative influence of parents. Attribute prejudices, mental blocks, and retarding of children to suppressive influence of parents. Infiltrate the churches and . . . discredit the Bible and emphasize the need for intellectual maturity which does not need a "religious church."[1]

It's sobering, my friend. The war is real. There's a world system focused on diverting our children away from God's truth. The enemy's plan is to kill, steal, and destroy children and he's ruthless in his pursuit of that goal. But remember, our children belong to God and as parents we are their caretakers and we need not fight this war alone. We have weapons of warfare that are mighty in God to pull down the enemy's strongholds. As it relates to our kids, strongholds are areas where the enemy has gained a foothold. They range from certain attitudes to behavioral patterns to health issues. If our kids are older and have established strongholds, we as parents have the spiritual authority to pull them down. If our kids are younger, we can do battle to prevent strongholds from being established. Either way, we have the weapons and the power available to pull them down.

God Is Bigger than Any Agenda Against the Family

I can't help but think of the time in the Old Testament when the Lord opened the eyes of Elisha's servant. If you remember, the king of Syria was pretty

---

[1]Cleon Skousen, *The Naked Communist* (Salt Lake City, Utah: Ensign Publishing, 1961), 259.

upset with Elisha because God had given him a supernatural revelation about the Syrian's military plans
against Israel. After Elisha reported that information
to the king of Israel, the king of Syria was furious and
sought to destroy Elisha. One night, while Elisha and
his servant slept in their tent, the great army of Syria
came and completely surrounded them. Imagine that,
a whole army against two of God's servants!

I'm sure many parents reading this can relate. No
doubt you've often felt outnumbered as if whole armies
were coming against you and your children. When the
servant stepped out of his tent the next morning and
saw that they were surrounded he was terrified. So he
cried to Elisha, "Alas, my master! What shall we do?"
But instead of responding in fear, Elisha responded in
faith. "Do not fear," he said, "for those who are with us
are more than those who are with them." Did you get
that? Even though with the natural eye it *appeared*
that they were outnumbered, Elisha saw with the eyes
of faith and spoke the truth. Then Elisha prayed, "Lord,
open his eyes that he may see." The scripture says,
"Then the Lord opened the eyes of the young man, and
he saw. And behold, the mountain was full of horses
and chariots of fire all around Elisha" (2 Kings 6:8-18).

There you have it. Though it looked like certain
death in the natural, the truth was God's army was
present and far superior. When we are in the midst of
brutal battles for the destiny of our
children, it may appear and feel like
we are outnumbered, but the truth
is, God is in complete control and
we have a much bigger military
force on our side.

> ❧
>
> THE ENEMY HAS
> ABSOLUTELY *NO*
> AUTHORITY OVER
> OUR SEED.
>
> ❧

The enemy has absolutely *no*
authority over our seed. Proverbs

11:21 KJV says that *"the seed of the righteous shall be delivered."* God didn't say might be, or could be. He said "<u>shall be</u> delivered." It is God's will that as righteous believers our children, our seed, be delivered from evil, delivered from the hand of the enemy. That includes drugs, alcohol, immorality, homosexuality, and all forms of perversion. But it doesn't happen automatically. It requires the leadership of godly parents.

Serious Business

The point I'm making here is that being a parent is serious business. It's not a role to be taken lightly. And if you are a parent and you are a Christian, then you *are* called. Whether you know it or not, whether you understand it or not, the calling to raise champions for God is upon you. Many children in the world are perishing because of their parents' lack of knowledge and failure to realize the seriousness of their calling. Millions upon millions of children have perished because their parents had no knowledge of why they were parents and why they had kids. Parents have a responsibility to train their children in the way of the Lord.

Parenting can be a difficult task and maybe in the past you have felt tired, frustrated, or even like a failure, but there is power to do the job and do it well. It is in our weakness that He is made strong. God will give you the strength to be the parent that He has called you to be. No parent can ever be successful without the constant flow of God's grace and mercy upon them. It takes supernatural power to raise godly seed.

Raising champions for Him will take a deeper commitment than the average parent. It will take a determination to persevere. The task calls for a tough faith because it involves some hard things like change,

6

effort, time, prayer, meditation in the Word, and unrelenting resolve. Lamentations 2:19 says, *"Pour out your heart like water before the face of the Lord. Lift your hands toward Him for the life of your young children."* This scripture becomes the guide for the parent wishing to raise champions for God. They pour themselves out to God on behalf of their children. Their purpose is no longer their own, but now is from God, for God, and to God. They are entering a divine partnership with Him.

The Standard: God's Word

Two of the major problems with modern-day parenting are a sense of randomness and a lack of vision. It's a kind of "whatever will be, will be" attitude—parents who are just going along with the flow, allowing the world system to have more and more influence on their children. When parents do not have a clear, godly vision for their children, they find themselves wandering around watching what everybody else is doing. But when a parent *knows* where they are going and *knows* what they are going after, they are then motivated and empowered each day to do whatever it takes

> TWO OF THE MAJOR
> PROBLEMS WITH MODERN-
> DAY PARENTING ARE A
> SENSE OF RANDOMNESS
> AND A LACK OF VISION.

to see God's desire fulfilled. They have a standard, the plumb line of God's Word, to gauge themselves and their children.

You have God on your side and the end result is not random chance. God's Word will win out. The following testimony from our son Paul helps illustrate God's faithfulness to bring His Word to our children's mind when it's been instilled into them. I'll let Paul tell you in his own words.

Teenagers these days seem to get everything they want. It's kind of an impatient generation, and everything is at the click of the mouse on the Internet. They don't have CDs anymore; they've got iPods. All of this stuff is just right there in their hands.

In my parents' generation, they had to work for stuff and be patient to get it. That's what they taught me growing up.

They began to speak the Word of God to me, and there would be times where I just did not want to hear the Word. I would roll my eyes or walk away, but they continued to speak the Word into my life. Because of that, whenever I hit a faith crisis—a time in my life when I wasn't sure why something happened or when everything that I had learned growing up all of a sudden was challenged—I remembered the words they spoke into my life.

My sisters, brother, and I are the seeds that came from my parents. Many of you have a seed and it's your children and your grandchildren. You have to water your seeds. You have to take care of them. And you have to cultivate them in order for them to grow healthy. You've got to water them and you've got to do the right thing.

My parents taught us to have good standards and morals in our lives. When we got to high school, our friends started telling us about different things, and I went into shock mode. I didn't know a whole lot. It seemed that I was in a bubble until about age sixteen, and then I was like, "What is that word?" And my friends laughed at me and said, "Paul, you are so sheltered." But it was good because when I got to that stage of life, it was like I was pure.

And when I got to college, I hit a faith crisis in my freshman year because people began to question my faith and people really came down on a lot of stuff that our family stands for and were really critical about it. It was hard. I was thinking, "Everything that I've learned is now being torn in two. What am I supposed to do?" And I remembered the words they spoke into my life, and I remembered the mission trips that they sent me on.

Mom and Dad taught us not to take shortcuts and they taught us just to be thankful for what we've been given and what we've worked for. When I turned sixteen, my parents didn't buy me a car. I had to buy it myself, pay the insurance, and buy the gas. But they did buy me a ticket on a mission trip.

In order for this next generation not to be destroyed and corrupted, we've got to start planting those seeds of the Word and start connecting with them. Whether they roll their eyes at you or walk away, continue to plant the Word in their life.

Your kids may not always understand or even like it when you are training them by God's standard. But when you are committed to raising champions for Him, the standard is laid down, the goals are established, and every part of your being is set like a flint, determined to achieve God's best. Your goals have become tied to Him. You've answered "yes" to the higher calling and have sided with the God of the universe. His power is readily available for the task.

Your Child's Greatest Need: Jesus

Your child's greatest need is Jesus. You see, regardless of how sweet and compliant they may be, all children are born in sin, separated from God with an indwelling sin nature. In John 3:6-7 Jesus said to Nicodemus, *"That which is born of the flesh is flesh, and that which is born of the Spirit is spirit . . . [Therefore,] you must be born again."*

"Born of the flesh" here means born into sin. Having been born of flesh our children are carnal in their nature. Romans 8:7-8 clearly says, *"The carnal mind is enmity against God; for it is not subject to the law of God, nor indeed can be. So then, those who are in the flesh cannot please God."* Whether we like it or not, that is an adequate description of our children—until they are born again.

This means that our top priority as parents raising champions is to be an evangelist in our home. We need to teach our children and grandchildren about Jesus. Show them Jesus. Give them Jesus. They must see and understand their need for a Savior. If they grow up without a clear and simple knowledge of their need for salvation, we will have failed in our primary task as their spiritual leader.

While it is true that our child's salvation is ultimately a matter between them and God, as parents, we are nonetheless responsible for exalting Christ in our homes and pointing them to Jesus as the one and only Savior. Romans 10:14 says, *"How shall they believe in Him of whom they have not heard? And how shall they hear without a preacher?"* As Christian parents, we are

10

the first and most important evangelists God has given them and they are watching our lives up close to see whether we really believe what we preach. The good news is, as I stated in Chapter 5, children are amazingly open and receptive to the things of God and the earlier we can tell them about the Lord, the better.

In the apartment outreach crusades we held many years ago, we generally had more children than adults, and there were usually more children saved than adults. There's a reason: *"For of such is the kingdom of heaven"* (Matthew 19:14). Children are easier to reach. If you tell them Jesus died for them, most of them will receive Him gladly. If you tell an adult that Jesus died for them, often they'll say, "Let me think about it. I'm not ready yet. I'm not into that stuff."

Dwight L. Moody, a great man of God of years past, was once asked how many people were saved in a particular meeting. He said, "Three and a half." Someone asked, "Oh, you had a child saved?" He said, "No, I had three children and one adult! The adult's life is half gone."

One of the reasons our church, Victory Christian Center in Tulsa, Oklahoma, is reaching out to little children in the children's ministry, in the bus ministry, mobile kidz clubs and in crusades is because it's better to save a life and prevent a child from going wrong than it is to try to rehabilitate him later. If you reach your children at a young age, you can see their lives continue to grow in God. If they are older, God can still do miracles. We've seen it over and over again!

Today God wants to fill you with His love and empower you by the Spirit. He is equipping you with the Word of God so that you *can* go out and fulfill your holy assignment to raise up godly seed.

FAITH IN ACTION

If you take your calling to parenthood seriously, then pray the following prayer: Lord, please help me to see the awesome responsibility and privilege that You have bestowed upon me as a parent. It's an honor and a holy calling to raise my children to be champions for You. I make a fresh commitment today to invest myself into my family and my church family. I choose to stand on Your promises concerning my children. Lord, grant me the wisdom, direction, and strength that I will need in order to be a godly parent. Lord, I know I can only be successful through Your power and help. I depend completely on You to enable me to raise champions for You.

_____

Signature

_____

Date

"Come, you children, listen to me; I will teach you the fear of the Lord" Psalm 34:11.

"'No weapon formed against you [or against your children] *shall prosper, and every tongue which rises against you in judgment you shall condemn. This is the heritage of the servants of the Lord, and their righteousness is from Me,' says the Lord"* Isaiah 54:17.

2

FRAMING OUR CHILDREN
WITH THE WORD OF GOD

*"For all the promises of God in Him are Yes,
and in Him Amen, to the glory of God through us."*
— 2 Corinthians 1:20

God never makes a promise that He can't or won't back up. When He promises something you can bank on it because He always says "yes" to it. In fact, God never makes a promise that He won't keep. Not keeping His promise would go directly against His nature. Titus 1:2 KJV tells us plainly that God cannot lie, *"In hope of eternal life, which God, that cannot lie, promised before the world began."* So, we *can* know for certain that the things God has promised to us in His Word *are* His will for our lives.

៚

OUR FAITH RESTS ON
GOD'S WORD—
WHAT HE SAYS,
NOT WHAT WE SEE.

៚

There are many promises in the Bible, and they're all written for our benefit, just waiting to be believed and acted upon. And when you find the promises relating to your children, you need to know that God says "yes" to them and that He *will* perform them. Our faith rests on God's Word—what He says, not what we see.

The Worlds Were Framed by the Word of God

Hebrews 11:3 explains that, *"By faith we understand that the worlds were <u>framed</u> by the word of God, so that the things which are seen were not made of things which are visible."*

Many years ago God gave me a revelation concerning this scripture. I'd heard it many times before, yet on that day, something clicked inside my spirit about how it could be applied to the family and children.

When God spoke the worlds into existence the scripture says He framed them with His Word so that the things that are visible were made out of things that were invisible—not seen. What came to be seen in reality was made out of things not seen. When faith rose up out of God's Spirit, He spoke it and the worlds came into being. When God spoke the word LIGHT, there was LIGHT. When He spoke the word EARTH, there was EARTH. When we look around us today and observe the incredible beauty of creation, we understand that God created it all with His Word.

God believed it, spoke it, and by His Word, the colors, the flowers, the bees, and everything in creation from the smallest atom to the farthest galaxy, from DNA to the human brain—everything came into existence. God framed it all with His Word. When I understood this, I then saw it in my spirit. I had the revelation. We must frame our families with the Word of God—frame our children with what God says about them, not what we see.

Speak God's Word
Over Your Family

How do we do it? How do we frame our children with the Word of God? We begin by saying out loud, "My family is blessed. My family is redeemed. Our children are anointed. They are set free. They walk in victory." We begin to confess the promises of God for our children.

Let me ask you a question. What frame have you put your family in? I ask that question because many people really don't have a clue. Their words are something to the tune of, "Well, you know. We're just. I don't know what's gonna happen to these kids." And I see parents talking about how their kids are spoiled rotten, how bad they are, and how difficult they are. But what are they doing? They're framing their children with negative words instead of God's Word.

Let me tell you something. If someone says destructive things over your children that are contrary to what God's Word says, you tell them, "NO! Our children are blessed in righteousness." I can't tell you how many times I've stopped people right in their tracks when they've spoken negative things over our children or other children in other families. After I confronted them about it, they'd just stand there shocked and bewildered, not knowing how to respond. Then, I'd just calmly tell them, "Look, God's Word says our children are blessed, so we don't let people say those destructive things over them."

15

Don't let them say destructive things over yours either. Even if it is Grandma! Teach Grandma to talk faith. It doesn't matter who it is. If you're going to raise champions for God you have to take a stand. Frame your children with God's Word, with His promises. Not with what you see but with what you believe. This is where most parents miss it. They see their child act a certain way and then begin to speak what they are acting like. That's not faith.

Consider this: Back in Hebrews 11:3, what if God had spoken what He had seen? What if He had declared the darkness? God would have looked out over the darkness and void and would have said something like, "There sure is a lot of darkness out there. Everything is so void and empty. I don't have anything to work with." And you know what the end result would have been? Darkness. Nothingness. Void.

We Are to be Imitators of God

Instead, when God looked out over the darkness He didn't call it darkness. He said, "Let there be light!" He spoke into existence what He desired. By that same spirit of faith frame your children and family with the Word of God. Romans 4:17 gives some further illumination on this. ". . . *God, who gives life to the dead and calls those things which do not exist as though they did.*" Did you get that? God calls the things that do not exist as though they did. Ephesians 5:1 tells us to be *"imitators of God."* We imitate God by doing what He did. It's not me or my opinion. It's the Word of God.

Raising champion children requires talking to them as though they already *are* what God says about them. "Thank You, Lord, that my children are joyful and peaceful." They may be running all over the house

16

screaming and throwing stuff and breaking things! Regardless of what's going on in the natural, just keep on declaring God's promises. "Lord, I thank You my children are taught of You and great is their peace." We may not be seeing any outward manifestations in them, but nevertheless, changes are occurring in their spirits and will one day come to the surface. Never underestimate the power of speaking words of faith over your children. The words of faith that you speak over them now *will* come out of them and sustain them in times of crisis.

> REGARDLESS OF WHAT'S GOING ON IN THE NATURAL, JUST KEEP ON DECLARING GOD'S PROMISES.

You see, faith believes with the heart. It is when, deep inside your core, you actually believe what God said about your children is true. And it is so true that you are going to dare to speak it every day. Luke 6:45 declares, *"Out of the abundance of the heart his mouth speaks."* If you really believe what is in your heart, then you speak it out of your mouth. A declaration is made, a statement of faith.

> LUKE 6:45 DECLARES, "OUT OF THE ABUNDANCE OF THE HEART HIS MOUTH SPEAKS."

The Challenge to Parents

My challenge to you, as a parent, is that you not only read the promises of God for your children, and pray them daily, but you speak them regularly. Frame your family with God's Word, with words of faith. When we do this, there's no more random chance or "whatever will be, will be." No, sir, you're praying and speaking them by faith onto a path of righteousness.

You're standing your ground with the shield of faith about your children. You're keeping the enemy from stealing, killing, or destroying your child's destiny. Obviously you must correct and discipline in line with what you are speaking and we will cover this in more depth later in the book. Remember, God's on your side! You have His promises and if God is for you, who can be against you?[2]

Second Peter 1:4 declares, "*By which have been given to us exceedingly great and precious promises, that through these you may be partakers of the divine nature, having escaped the corruption that is in the world. . . .*" This scripture brings out two important points that are absolutely imperative to understand if we are going to be effective as parents. According to the above passage, it's through the great and precious promises of God that we get His divine nature inside of us. Then, not only do we get to be partakers of His divine nature, but it's through the promises of God that we escape the corruption that is in this world.

We believe, speak, and pray the promises of God because in doing so His divine nature is imparted to us and we escape the corruption that's in the world. Second Corinthians 4:13 tells us that, "*. . . since we have the same spirit of faith, according to what is written, 'I believed and therefore I spoke,' we also believe and therefore speak.*"

When we declare the promises of God by faith we are doing two things. First, we are *believing* what they say. Second, we are *speaking* what they say. Where there's no belief and no confession, there's no power. So, it's not whether you know it or read it. It's whether you believe it, and speak it, and act upon it.

---

[2]Romans 8:31.

When we see our children doing something negative and contrary to what we believe, at that point, we have a choice to either speak what we see, or by faith, to call things that are not as though they already exist. Faith language speaks what God says rather than natural circumstances.

By Faith

≈

WHEN WE SEE OUR CHILDREN DOING SOMETHING NEGATIVE AND CONTRARY TO WHAT WE BELIEVE, AT THAT POINT, WE HAVE A CHOICE TO EITHER SPEAK WHAT WE SEE, OR BY FAITH, TO CALL THINGS THAT ARE NOT AS THOUGH THEY ALREADY EXIST.

≈

Let me ask you this: How does a person say, "Jesus is Lord" and get saved when they are a sinner? They say it by faith. When we first got saved, we were lost and undone sinners without Christ. But someone told us, or we read it in the Bible, that Jesus died for us and was raised from the dead and that through believing in Him and confessing Him as Lord we would be saved and the Holy Spirit would come live inside of us. So, *by faith* we believed, prayed, and agreed with what God said. We prayed, "Jesus, I believe that You died for my sins, were buried, rose again, and are alive. I receive You as my Lord and Savior and I declare today You are my Lord." And in that one moment, we called something that was not as though it was and it came into existence. In an instant, the Holy Spirit came inside.

However, even though everything that happened was true, it took time for the evidence of that fact to work its way out in our daily lives. The longer we stayed with our confession and declared Jesus as our Lord, day by day we became, and are still becoming, more conformed to Christ's image. Little by little, more and more of the old junk is falling off our lives. We're no longer ruled by sin and darkness. Instead we are ruled by life and peace and it all began with a moment's confession of faith.

James 2:26 says, "... *faith without works is dead.*" In other words, faith is all about believing God, speaking His Word, and taking action. The core of faith is God's Word—that we hear it, believe it, speak it, and act upon it. Begin to declare with your mouth, "*The Spirit of God is being poured out on my children. God is pouring His blessing and His goodness upon my offspring.*"

Now, understand this; the enemy wants children and he wants us talking about what is happening in the natural. He wants us to declare what we see, what people have said, or what we feel. He wants us to say the opposite of what God's Word says. The enemy knows that "*without faith it is impossible to please* [God]. ...*"*[3] So, if he can get us to confess what we see and to walk in doubt, he knows we can't gain the victory. If he can get us to agree with the circumstances, then the promises are not going to be effective in our lives or in the lives of our children.

John's Testimony of Faith

In this book we have tried to insert as many personal examples as possible. The following is another testimony from one of our children that illustrates the power of framing our children with God's Word and how that works out in their everyday lives. This one is from John.

Paul and I started mowing yards somewhere around the 5th or 6th grade. My dad had the idea that we needed to work. He thought that if we

---

[3]Hebrews 11:6.

worked hard and made money from working, we'd learn more about life and stuff like that. My dad convinced us that the only way to do that was by mowing yards. He actually had a lot of other ideas for us to make money, but he said, "You know what? You guys need to start out mowing yards."

It was really a great experience. I learned how to socialize with so many types of people because we had lawns on the north side and lawns on the south side of Tulsa—two completely different groups of people. By the 7th grade we had built up to having eight yards to mow, but by the summer before my senior year, we had twenty-two yards to mow. We were making great money.

One Saturday Paul and I were out mowing lawns in a newly built neighborhood. This builder had about five or six homes that he had built, and he let us mow all the yards at those vacant houses. As Paul was weed-eating the front yard that day, I was mowing the lawn. The grass was wet and thick, so I had to stop every few seconds and clean out my lawn mower. Well, I started thinking, "There has got to be a faster way to do this." So, while I was mowing, I would just keep the motor running, tilt up the mower, and reach my hand in this side plastic funnel and pull out the grass. I even got a little stick to help me pull the grass out. However, the stick got stuck one time, so I reached up into the funnel (without even thinking). My brother was watching me, and I reached all the way up in there. There was this THUD, and I knew something was wrong. I pulled my hand out, and there was

21

*blood everywhere. The tip of my middle finger—
from my knuckle up on my middle finger—was
just dangling. I was in so much shock that I didn't
feel the pain yet.*

*Paul just started freaking out. He started cry-
ing. I wasn't even crying yet, because I didn't feel
any pain. Paul hurried to try to get help for me,
but since it was a newly built neighborhood, no
one lived in the houses. Here he was—going from
house to house, beating on the doors, crying,
"HELP! My brother needs help!"*

*I finally got his attention and said, "Paul, no
one lives in these houses. Can you please get on
the phone and call 9-1-1 or something?" So he
called 9-1-1. While I was waiting for an emer-
gency vehicle to get there, I went to the side of the
house and turned on the water to rinse off the
blood. As I was holding my hand underneath the
faucet, the water finally came out with such force
that the tip of my finger fell off onto the ground.
I picked it up. By this time, I was flipping out.
Then Paul was flipping out. A neighbor from an
adjoining neighborhood came by, and I put the
fingertip on a bowl of ice. I was just looking at
my detached finger. That was really weird.*

*The ambulance finally came, and the atten-
dant said, "It may affect the nerves in the rest of
your finger. We may have to take off your finger."
And I just said, "I rebuke you, in the name of
Jesus!" He said, "Excuse me?" I realized how
that might have sounded, and I said, "I don't
rebuke you. I rebuke what you said. That's
wrong. I am going to keep my finger." And they
were able to reattach the fingertip. Today, I have*

full function in the finger. It was definitely a learning experience.

The truth is, when we declare the promises of God and confess them for and over our children, we are framing them in the Word of God—in what God says about them. By making these confessions daily and standing upon the promises of God's Word, we are taking positive steps of action. You are also training your children how to speak faith themselves and respond with the Word of God to negative circumstances they face.

જે

WHEN WE DECLARE THE PROMISES OF GOD AND CONFESS THEM FOR AND OVER OUR CHILDREN, WE ARE FRAMING THEM IN THE WORD OF GOD—IN WHAT GOD SAYS ABOUT THEM.

જે

When thoughts of anxiety and fear try to take over, take control by confessing the promises. With God's Word in our hearts and confessing it with our lips we can claim our children for God's Kingdom and confidently expect God to honor His promises!

FAITH IN ACTION

In the space provided below, write down the names of your children and any other special information about them that you would like to pray over them.

My Champions for God

1)_____
2)_____
3)_____
4)_____
5)_____
6)_____
7)_____
8)_____

After you have written them down, call forth the Word of God over each one of them by name. Use the following scripture promises as a guide. These are just some of my favorites. Remember, there are many promises in the Bible! Get into the habit of doing this daily.

"'All your children shall be taught by the Lord, . . . no weapon formed against you [or against your children] *shall prosper, and every tongue which rises against you in judgment you shall condemn. This is the heritage of the servants of the Lord, and their righteousness is from Me,' says the Lord"* Isaiah 54:13,17.

"But thus says the Lord: 'Even the captives of the mighty shall be taken away, and the prey of the terrible be delivered; for I will contend with him who contends with you, and I will save your children'" Isaiah 49:25.

"Praise the Lord! Blessed is the man who fears the Lord, who delights greatly in His commandments. His

descendants *will be mighty on earth; the generation of the upright will be blessed"* Psalm 112:1-2.

"But the mercy of the Lord is from everlasting to everlasting on those who fear Him, and His righteousness to children's children, to such as keep His covenant, and to those who remember His commandments to do them" Psalm 103:17-18.

"They shall not labor in vain, nor bring forth children for trouble; for they shall be the descendants of the blessed of the Lord, and their offspring with them" Isaiah 65:23.

"The righteous man walks in his integrity; his children are blessed after him" Proverbs 20:7.

3

No More Jekyll & Hyde Christianity

". . . Let us lay aside every weight, and the sin which so easily ensnares us, and let us run with endurance the race that is set before us."
— Hebrews 12:1

When raising champions for God, authenticity in our personal walk with the Lord is imperative. There is no way we can live one way and expect our children to turn out another way. It simply won't work. Our walk must match our talk. Faith can't be merely a show where we put on a church face on Sundays and then take it off the rest of the week. Doing that may fool some church folk, but I guarantee it won't fool the kids. Kids have this innate ability to see right through fake.

If we are going to reach our goal of raising champions for God, then the days of Jekyll & Hyde Christianity are over. It's going to take deeply committed, surrendered lives, and reaching a place in our own spiritual lives that our faith impacts our children. There's no other way. Hypocrisy nullifies the impact of our words. I repeat. Hypocrisy nullifies the impact of our words.

The Buck Stops with Us!

So often people want to put the responsibility of raising their kids on everybody else—the churches, the schools, even their spouses. But to be effective with our kids, the buck has to stop with us! We must take personal responsibility. You must ask yourself the following question. *"Am I living a life that is exemplary for my children to follow?"* I realize that none of us are perfect and we will make mistakes. I'm not talking about "pie in the sky" religiosity. I am talking about you having a real and authentic walk with God—that your faith is alive, active, and relevant. You can't expect your children to love God if you yourself are lukewarm, halfhearted, and half-baked in your Christianity. They *will* be the same way. The way to prevent your kids from disrespecting you and for them to honor God is for there to be a genuine fire of faith burning inside you that's evident in the home, at the grocery store, at their school functions, and everywhere you go, not just in the church. It's a faith that governs every aspect of your life.

If we don't have an active prayer life, why should they? If we don't read and study the Bible, why should they? If we don't worship God acceptably with reverence and awe, why should they? Children often imitate their parents. Can you see yourself in them? If actions don't match words children will often become cynical toward their parents. Children are watching their parents and listening to parents' conversation, and they are watching how we respond to difficulty and trials. Are we responding in faith? Are we worshiping at home? Do we rejoice in the Lord there? Well, they're watching us. They're watching the way we drive in traffic—our response to the guy who rudely pulled out in front of us or what we're uttering when we're being held up by a slower driver. Yes, they're watching us and they will model what they see. Raising champions means modeling the life we want our children to live. Live it so they can see it.

❧

RAISING CHAMPIONS MEANS MODELING THE LIFE WE WANT OUR CHILDREN TO LIVE. LIVE IT SO THEY CAN SEE IT.

❧

Think about your words. Do they speak criticism? Do they trash other people? Are they degrading and demeaning to your spouse? I've heard parents shout to their kids, "Watch your mouth," but then they turn around and cuss the wallpaper off the walls! We can preach to our kids all day long about what they should be doing, but what they are learning is what we are confessing and then walking out.

We founded Victory Christian School back in 1979. Since then we have seen hundreds of kids go through and let me tell you something; when you have a school you learn a lot about kids, but you learn just as much about parents. You'd be amazed at how many parents we learned were falsifying information, lying in reports and responses they've given to us and their kids knew all about it. Then, some of those same parents would complain and get upset when their children acted in ways they didn't approve. Hello? Is anybody home? If you want to raise children to be truth tellers, then tell the truth. It's not rocket science.

Years ago when we were in the market for a new home, the realtor showed us a house that happened be owned by a couple whose kids attended our school. They'd moved out, but had left some furniture which included their TV and video collection. I'll never forget our young children opening the door of the video cabinet and being shocked at what they saw. Sharon and I had to quickly shut the door because of all the adult-rated movies with ungodly images on the cases! Sharon and I had to explain those videos to our children. "How could they do that, Daddy?" they asked me. "Well, kids, not everybody has the same standards."

Afterwards, I thought about what had occurred. This couple had put their kids in our Christian school, but their life at home was completely at odds with what we stood for at the school and church.

Are You Living What You Preach?

Over the years, I've been amazed at those who bring their children to our youth ministers and teachers at school wanting them to raise their kids for them, but at home they're doing drugs or living out of wedlock, etc. Trust me on this; you can bring your children to church and you can put them in a Christian school, but if you are not living what you preach at home it's nullifying it! If you are serious about raising champions for God, then things are going to have to be different at home. Now, if you just want to raise kids, then go ahead and do like everybody else does. But God is calling us to a higher standard.

How about pornography in the house? Do you have a block on the Internet? I remember a lady came in for counseling one time who had some pornography going on in her home that involved the Internet. She just took a chair and crashed in the whole thing! She fixed it. I'm not advocating smashing your spouse's computer with a chair. There are different ways to fix situations, but you do need to take action. And if it requires smashing a computer, well, do what you have to do. However, the biggest thing that needs to happen in raising champion children is what happens on the inside of us because how we live really does have an impact upon our children. Listen to what our daughter Ruthie says about it.

My mom and dad have always walked out the Word of God. Even if they said or did something that was out of line, they would immediately apologize to us and ask for our forgiveness. They never acted like they were above having to repent. They walked humbly, which I believe is why I had such a strong relationship with God through my teenage years and still do today. I saw the realness in them. It was not a fake Christianity. If they messed up, they admitted it.

If they could not make it to one of our events, they would not promise to be there. They would call us and encourage us. They never wanted to break a promise, and that spoke loudly to me. They honored their word. When they said they would be there, they were there. They attended many soccer games, piano recitals, basketball games, choir programs, plays, football games, and baseball games. They showed us that even though they were in the ministry, they still had time for their kids.

Spending time with us was a way they demonstrated their love for us. As little girls,

Sarah and I liked to do hair, so we put my dad's hair in fifty barrettes. He just let us do it, and we have the pictures to prove it!

We liked going to school with Mom. She would take us to the donut shop on the way to school. That was her way of doing something with us that didn't cost much, and it was something we enjoyed. It didn't matter what it was. What mattered was the time they took to spend with us. There may not always be time to sit down at home to be with your kids, but you can take them with you to run errands and use that time to invest into them.

This also went into the ministry. They took us on the mission field even when we were young. When my parents went to Russia every month for eighteen months straight, they would take one of us with them each time they went. I went to Russia four times by myself with my parents. During that season of our lives we each had the opportunity to spend alone time with Mom and Dad. This was a special event that became a regular occurrence when they went to other countries to hold crusades. They put us in positions to minister alongside them by having us sing, speak a few moments to the people, and allowing us to go out in the crowd to pray for people. We loved being a part of the ministry at a young age.

When we were younger, Victory Christian Center had apartment crusades in the government housing of Tulsa one weekend a month. On that Friday night we all went as a family to the apartment crusade. We would go door-to-door *with my parents, inviting people to come to the meeting and sharing the love of Jesus with them. I remember wanting to have friends over to spend the night on Friday. I wanted to do something fun with them. My parents told me that I could have friends over, but we were still going to the crusade. At first I was embarrassed and upset that we had to go to an outreach on the night that I wanted to have fun with my friends, but as I went that night I saw that I could have fun with my friends by ministering to people. I realized it was all in my attitude, and if my friends couldn't find joy in helping people, then I needed to reevaluate my friendships. Out of those experiences, one of my friends and I got involved in other areas of the church together. Our friendship was strengthened because we based it on giving out of ourselves.*

All people need love, and my parents taught me that by loving everyone. It wasn't just about being nice to people at church or being behind a platform and saying "we love you" and then leaving. It was and still is their life. I'm in ministry today because I saw that integrity in both of my parents. It didn't matter the status of a person— whether they were middle class, upper class, lower class, or somewhere in between, whatever income they had—they loved that person. Out of that, it instilled inside of us a love for all kinds of people. We saw that in them and believed that we could be the same.

Mom and Dad live what they preach. They spent time with us. They instilled faith and the Word of God in us. I believe that was what caused me to be in the ministry and love and serve God.

God *Is* a God of Grace

We made a lot of mistakes and had to repent before our children. I also realize, as I've said, that all parents make mistakes. God is a God of grace who can miraculously redeem the time lost. He can work all things out for our good. Yet, we must understand that we are living in a day and age where compromise and lukewarmness have seeped into the church and people want one standard for their kids, but they themselves want to live by another standard. And it simply does not work. Our kids see right through the facades. You need to decide right now. Do you really want your kids to be champions? Do you really want to do what it takes? I ask those questions because your children are going to rise to the level of where you are. If you desire them to live at a higher level of righteousness, purity, victory, and joy—for them to desire godly spouses and have marriages that succeed—then you'll be willing to lay aside the weights and sins that are hindering you and run the race set before you.

Certainly, all of us have had sins and weights to lay aside, to confess and be cleansed of. We've made mistakes and had bad habits that were weighing us down and keeping us from having a stronger relationship with God and from being more effective parents. What's important is from this day forward to say, "Lord, with Your help, with Your grace and mercy, I am going to deal with these issues and then be the best example I can be!" Remember, we produce after our own kind and we want to be the kind who raise champions!

FAITH IN ACTION

Take some time to reflect and pray. With a pen and paper in hand, ask God to reveal to you any areas of your life that you need to deal with. Write them down so you can pray daily for them. Sins are obvious, but weights are things that may not necessarily be sin. They are areas of our lives—attitudes, strongholds, issues—that are hindering us from being the person God wants us to be and therefore are negatively affecting our ability to raise champions.

Areas That May Be Holding Me Back

1. _____

2. _____

3. _____

4. _____

"We do not want you to become lazy, but to imitate those who through faith and patience inherit what has been promised" Hebrews 6:12 NIV.

"Do not merely listen to the word, and so deceive yourselves. Do what it says" James 1:22 NIV.

"If we claim to be without sin, we deceive ourselves and the truth is not in us. If we confess our sins, he is faithful and just to forgive us our sins and to purify us from all unrighteousness" 1 John 1:8-9 NIV.

"Let the wicked forsake his way, and the unrighteous man his thoughts; let him return to the Lord, and He will have mercy on him; and to our God, for He will abundantly pardon" Isaiah 55:7.

"The people who know their God shall be strong, and carry out great exploits" Daniel 11:32.

HOW DO YOU SPELL LOVE?

"See then that you walk circumspectly, not as fools but as wise, redeeming the time, because the days are evil."
— *Ephesians 5:15-16*

I want to focus a moment on the importance of time and how the use of it applies to our relationship with God and our relationship with our children. Time is one of the most valued commodities that we possess. It's a gift more valuable than money and more precious than any material thing we own. When even a second of our time is lost, it's gone forever never to be gotten back. Therefore, we must treat our time with great thoughtfulness.

The word "circumspectly" in the above passage simply means *cautiously.* The Apostle Paul is exhorting us to conduct our lives in a very careful and attentive manner applying wisdom to our steps and to redeem our time. The word "redeeming" here actually means to make the most of every opportunity, to not squander occasions and openings that the Lord brings our way. He's warning us to be alert and not to waste our time but rather to use it wisely. In other words, the choices we make about the use of our time are very serious matters not to be taken lightly. If we are not intentional with our steps and our time, then our walk with God will suffer and our relationship with our children will suffer also.

As a pastor of a church I understand all too well the importance of managing time. If we are serious about our walk with God and about completing the work God has called us to as parents to raise champion children, then we must become intentional and disciplined in our use of time. There *is* enough time. It simply requires restructuring our priorities.

In Chapter 1, we established that if you are a Christian and if you are a parent, then you *are* called to the task of raising champions for God. Now, accepting that calling or rejecting it is up to you, but make no mistake about it, you *are* called. And think about this; within this awesome calling God has given us a tremendous opportunity, an occasion and opening to join with Him in the noble work of shaping and molding the lives of other human beings—our children. What an honor! What a privilege! However, it's an opportunity that God fully expects us to make the most of.

Time is short, friend, very short. The Bible says in Psalm 89:47 NIV that it's "fleeting." James 4:14 says, ". . . *For what is your life? It is even a vapor that appears for a little time and then vanishes away."* Think about it. If who and what we give our money to is important, how much more important is it who we give our time to? If we don't discipline ourselves in the use of our time for building lifelong relationships with our children, training them up in the ways of the Lord, then the time and opportunity will vanish before our very eyes. However, when we choose to invest our time into our children in order to raise them as champions for God, the rewards will be great not only in this life, but also in the life to come.

There is no greater gift you can give to your children than the gift of your time. It has been said that love is spelled T-I-M-E. When a child knows that you really care enough to spend time with them, then they will care also. Every quality moment you spend with your children is another building block in the foundation of their lives. It's also creating a strong relationship between you that will help with leading and disciplining them in the future.

&

LOVE IS SPELLED
T-I-M-E.

&

Quality Time

Now there are many different ways to redeem time with our children. It's not hard and may call for a little bit of creativity, but most importantly it calls for availability. The following are some effective ways to squeeze out more quality time with your kids, while at the same time building the character of God into them.

#1) Have fun with them. You know, parenting is not always about being serious. It's important that each of us find a way to laugh and have fun with our kids. Sometimes, especially in Christian families, everything with children is all solemn and stern, focused on one aspect. Now don't misunderstand me, parenting is serious business not to be taken lightly, but play is important too. Times of fun can turn into tremendous teaching opportunities. Kids are often more open and receptive when they are in the midst of fun activities.

❧

FUN IS SPENDING TIME WITH YOUR CHILD AND HAVING A LAUGH WITH THEM EVEN IF IT'S YOU THAT THEY'RE LAUGHING AT.

❧

We all need times to play and laugh together and what better way to show your child how much you love them and enjoy being with them than by having fun with them. Fun is spending time with your child and having a laugh with them even if it's you that they're laughing at. For example, with our girls I've had a lot of barrettes in my hair. Can you picture an adult man with his whole head covered with barrettes? What a sight I must have been! But, you know, the girls loved it. They would giggle and laugh and then give me hugs. So what if I looked funny. It was great and the memories it created will never be forgotten.

Another time, I remember was with the boys. They were always doing adventurous things and one Saturday, they put rubber bands around the handle of the kitchen sink sprayer holding it down. When the faucet is on, you squeeze in the handle and it sprays water. But they rubber banded the thing where the handle was pulled back and then turned and aimed it right at whoever would turn the faucet on. They forgot about it until Sunday morning. Well, Sharon was going to church and she was all dressed up, ready to go, but she needed to get a drink of water before she left. You get the picture. It was overflow!

Her hair was all sprayed. Well, it was funny, but it was also a little bit *not* funny because Sharon needed to get to church. She was already going to be late and then she had to blow dry her hair, put more makeup on, and change her clothes.

You know, Sharon could have gotten upset, but that's not what she did. She chose to go with it and have some fun. Even though it was adventurous and fun loving, they did receive correction and it never happened again.

When our kids were little there was a city park in the neighborhood with a community pool. In a city like ours, and in most towns, there's usually an opportunity to spend some quality time with your kids at public parks and facilities. We played all types of games, rode bikes together, played basketball, swam, and went on hikes. It was a constant thing with us depending on what time of the year it was. You did not have to have a lot of money, but we had many hours of fun. Today we still have lots of fun on vacations, only now there's more people involved.

Making quality time for our kids with activities like those down through the years was laying a foundation of love and bonding for our family. And again, it's amazing how many teachable moments presented themselves during these times of activity.

Here it is twenty-something years later and when our family gets together it's still a time of laughing, loving, and kidding each other where guards are down and everyone feels relaxed. Usually at least four or five people are talking at once and you're trying to keep up with which conversation is which. We call it "the Daugherty party." "We're going to have a Daugherty party!" Proverbs 17:22 KJV says, *"A merry heart doeth good like a medicine: but a broken spirit drieth the bones."* Laughter is good medicine. It brings healing to the body, mind, and spirit. Christian homes above all others should be filled with love and laughter.

Not long ago the boys and I were floating down the Buffalo National River in Arkansas and Paul asked me a question. "Dad," he said, "what are you doing these days for a hobby?" He'd just graduated from ORU and his nose had been in the books for the past few months. "Well, Paul," I said, "everything in the way of hobby or fun we've done through the years has been committed to you kids. You know I loved to camp and hunt and fish. That's what I did growing up, but when you kids came along, something got in me and your mom to invest our spare time into you guys. So, whatever you kids were doing, that became our hobbies. Soccer, football, basketball, family camping, fishing, and going together to the lake were how we invested our time."

Then Paul asked, "Do you regret that you didn't have a hobby that involved other men?" "Paul," I said, "I have absolutely no regrets. I have great kids and you all love God today. The investment was worth it. Who could ask for more?"

Of course, I'm not saying it's wrong to have a hobby. I'm just saying do whatever it takes to find the time to invest in your kids and have fun.

#2) Get involved in their learning process. Another way you are able to have time with them is in their learning process. I'm talking about doing homework and reading books to them. I know homework and reading books may not sound too thrilling, but it's an optimal time to pour into our kids and grandkids, because they want and need our help. Little children especially love for someone to read to them. Older children also enjoy being read to. Whether it is a science project or reading a book, spending time learning together strengthens the bond with our children.

Reading is a powerful tool for teaching about God because reading was designed by God. God uses reading to communicate to us. He chose to reveal His will and

His ways to us in written form, the Bible. This brings us to the next section.

#3) Pray and read the Word of God to them. Make it a priority to pray and read the Word of God as a family. It isn't hard once you get started. If you are committed to it, God will make the way to accomplish it. Remember, we are going to a higher standard. It is critical, even when they are too young to understand in the natural, to put into them the Word and prayer. Their spirit is receiving the power and the presence of God Almighty. Their mind will more quickly comprehend the truth as we speak early in their lives.

For us, the best time to pray and read as a family was at night. We'd have all four of them either in the bed with us or on the floor every night. That's how our nights ended. "Okay, kids, we're all going to come in here and pray and read the Word." We'd ask questions and required all of our kids to respond. Sometimes it's important to let the kids ask questions. I remember one time, I had preached on "Soaring Like the Eagles" and that night one of the younger kids wanted to know why the eagles were so sore. "What happened to the eagles, Daddy? Why are they so sore?" That's a funny illustration, but really, there's no easier way to pass on godly wisdom than by simply praying, reading the Word of God to them, and discussing it.

#4) Keep the doors of communication open. When we talk about time with our children, keeping the doors of communication open is absolutely essential in strengthening our relationships with them. By keeping the doors of communication open, I am talking about you being a person they feel "safe" coming to. As a parent, you want to be a refuge for them where they can feel comfortable and open talking to you without being criticized. And they need to feel comfortable correcting you at times if you need it. I got some good correction just recently from one of our kids, very respectfully. I needed more information to get the facts straight on an incident that had happened. Rather than leaving me making a wrong assumption, the correction helped me understand the situation accurately. I would have made a wrong decision without that corrective information.

One thing we do not want to do to our children is to close or crush their spirits. That's one of the things the Lord has dealt with us about, that in communicating with our kids we were not to attack them, but we were to correct gently when they needed it and pray for and speak good over them. Sometimes families create environments where there's a negativity that closes their child's spirit. The doors of communication are shut. It's just "yeah," "no," and "bye." And when they do have something to say, it's difficult.

I remember once when John was just a little thing, three or four. An architect, another guy, and I were in my church office looking at some plans for a building we were constructing. The plans were spread out all over the floor. Well, the door opened and it was John. I said, "Hey, John," and he just walked straight to me, trampling right over all the plans and crawled up in my lap. I held him and right there we had a little talk. It was after school and a teacher assistant had brought him there after kindergarten class.

> ☙
>
> IF OUR KIDS CAN'T COME TO US, THEY'RE GOING TO GO TO SOMEONE ELSE, SOMEONE WHO MAY HAVE ENTIRELY DIFFERENT VALUES THAN YOU.
>
> ☙

You may say, "Well, he interrupted." I say, "No, he was not an interruption." We had an open door policy with our kids from the time they were very young that they could always come to us if there was a need. And I believe in this day and hour, when our kids are facing so many situations they are going to need to be able to come to us for help. And let me tell you something. If our kids can't come to us, they're going to go to someone else, someone who may have entirely different values than you.

When we talk about the open doors of communication, we have to talk about the importance of being a good, attentive listener. Communication is a two-way street. When we are listening attentively, it is sending a message to our kids that they're important enough to have our undivided attention. Many problems can be solved and even prevented when we simply take the time to listen attentively.

> ❧
>
> WHEN WE ARE LISTENING ATTENTIVELY, IT IS SENDING A MESSAGE TO OUR KIDS THAT THEY'RE IMPORTANT.
>
> ❧

Four tips on listening

- Stop what you are doing. Put the newspaper down or turn the television off.

- Look at them in the eyes, giving them your full attention.

- Try to hear what is really being said. Sometimes there are issues under the surface.

- Comment on what you heard and ask questions drawing more out of them.

#5) Make an effort to attend their functions. Attending school functions and other important activities is an extremely important way to show your children how much you support them. Of course, there will be times when you have scheduling conflicts and valid reasons why you cannot attend. However, when you can go to events like Back-to-School Night, a play, or a music or sporting event, make the effort to be present. When our children see that we are interested in what *they* are interested in, then they'll be more interested in what we have to offer them.

Not long ago, I was scheduled to pray for an evening city council meeting, and I realized it was the same time as my little grandson Isaac's birthday event. It didn't take me long to make the decision to send someone else who could pray just as powerful a prayer. I knew that I could go another time, but you know what? Isaac only has a birthday once a year. I needed to be there for him. There are times when you have to make that commitment. If you hear from God that you are to miss an event with your children then you must obey God and simply trust that God will open the door for you at another time. Through the years we have had schedule situations that caused us to miss an event in which our children participated. However, we have worked to adjust the schedule whenever possible.

#6) It's never too late to start. If you didn't spend enough time with your kids when they were younger, it's not too late to begin a new tradition. A wise person once said, "The best time to plant a tree was twenty years ago. The second best time is today." Romans 8:28 says, *"And we know that all things work together for good to those who love God, to those who are the called according to His purpose."* I don't know how God does it, but He is able to take even our mistakes and work them for the good if we let Him. He can restore what the enemy has stolen.

This is an hour when we must make an extra effort to build our families on the power of God and watch with the anointing of the Holy Spirit against the enemy. Even if your children are grown, you still have authority in the realm of the spirit to pray for them and stand on the Word of God against the works of the enemy in their lives.

Author Larry Jones points out in his book *Keep Walking*:

[Secular] psychologists say that 90 percent of a human's personality is formed by age seven. Ninety percent of the decisions people make for the rest of their lives are based on behaviors they've learned by the time they enter the second grade.[4]

I believe the one thing that can change that statistic is the grace of God operating by the Word and the power of the Holy Spirit. That is the hope and the promise that we have for children who are above seven years of age, teens, and even adult children who you feel like are already out of control.

Over the years we have watched hundreds of people turn their lives over to Christ and be delivered and set free from wrong habits and get healed from hurts of their past. Never give up on even one of your children or grandchildren because we have living proof that people can come back out of the worst addictions and lifestyles. We've seen people delivered from the worst, most horrible things that you can imagine.

This is a day and age where we need to say, "Nothing is impossible." God's going to work miracles, signs, and wonders. But on the other end of the spectrum, it's time for us to pour into our children and give them our love by investing our time into them.

---

[4]*Larry Jones, Keep Walking: One Man's Journey to Feed the World One Child at a Time* (New York: NY: The Doubleday Broadway Publishing Group, a Division of Random House, Inc., 2007), 1.

FAITH IN ACTION

Spend some time in prayer and reflection about this chapter. Then, write down two or three areas where you are doing really well and then write two or three areas where you could improve. If you want, rate yourself on a scale of 1 to 10. And remember, when doing this, it's not about condemnation. It's about us rising to a higher level and going above and beyond where we've been.

Areas I'm Doing Well

1. _____

2. _____

3. _____

4. _____

5. _____

Areas I Need Improvement

1. _____

2. _____

3. _____

4. _____

5. _____

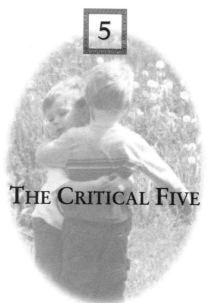

5

THE CRITICAL FIVE

"All your children shall be taught by the Lord,
and great shall be the peace of your children."
— Isaiah 54:13

Jesus said, *". . . whoever does not receive the kingdom of God as a little child will by no means enter it."*[5] He also said of children that *"of such is the kingdom of God"* (v.16). Someone with great faith is often said to have "childlike" faith. The obvious reason is because most children are wide open and receptive to the things of God. Like cool rain on a hot, parched day, children are refreshingly free of doubt, cynicism, and unbelief.

Without pride or the mental hang-ups that hold down so many adults, their minds are pliable. This is why it's critical to plant the seeds of God's Word and

---

[5]Luke 18:17.

godly principles into them as early as possible so that through their lives those seeds can germinate, take root, grow, and ultimately produce the sweet fruit of righteousness and peace. In addition to speaking the Word of God and teaching them godly principles, modeling godly behavior and protecting them from negative outside influences are ways of watering the godly seeds that have been planted in them.

Now, as we've previously established, the enemy also desires to get to children as early as possible in order to plant his seeds of corruption, pride, discord, rebellion, and addiction that ultimately produce destructive strongholds. Yes, a war for the souls of children is being waged and there are five critical arenas of influence where the battles are played out. For parents raising champions for God, it is in these five arenas that we must absolutely stand our ground, refuse to compromise, and maintain firm control. The critical five arenas are: the home, the church, the school, friends, and the media.

#1) The Home. Ideally, the home should be a place of unity, harmony, love, structure, order, and discipline— a refuge that is peaceful and supportive. Our children ought to feel safe at home regardless of what's going on in the outside world. If there is dissention between you and your spouse or between you and the school administration, leaders in the church, or leaders in authority, your children will know it. They are watching you and picking up on how you are in every aspect of your life.

Whether it's between you and your spouse or another person of authority, when disagreements do come up and things need to be discussed, those discussions shouldn't take place in front of the children.

There are certain situations and things that their ears are not prepared to hear. There is certain information that should only be shared between husband and wife. In the military there is a phrase about information called "need to know." Certain ranks only need to know certain information. The privates know what they need to know and that's it. As you move up the ladder each rank, sergeants, lieutenants, colonels, are privy to more "need to know information" and so it goes all the way up to the General. Guard with diligence what is being discussed in front of your children, particularly in the home.

Just as it does with our finances and other aspects of our lives, the law of sowing and reaping applies to the home. If there's anger and arguing in the home, then it poisons the atmosphere and infects our children. If we sow animosity and cynicism, we are going to reap animosity and cynicism with our kids. If we disrespect authority, they are going to disrespect us. Each of us must work hard to keep the home atmosphere positive and faith filled. And creating an environment of peace has nothing to do with economic levels. Whether you live in a trailer, a mansion, or a hut, your home can be a haven. We've been in some of the poorest places in the world, in Haiti, Sierra Leone, and India, yet there were homes where the love of God abounded and the families walked in harmony with the Holy Spirit. Despite poverty, they were homes of peace and encouragement. We have seen the very same in wealthy homes.

Another thing that is important in the home is appropriate touching and displays of affection. Home should be a place of many hugs where children are affirmed again and again that they are loved. If you want to communicate love and acceptance to your kids, you have to be willing to pull them close, hug them, and tell them that you love them. It's also vital, particularly for girls, that they understand what appropriate hugs are. If they are not touched appropriately, then they will seek affection elsewhere. Every child needs appropriate hugs of affirmation. When we talk about appropriate touching, it is important that we always respect each other's personal boundaries. Sometimes our children will not want to be hugged and we must respect those times.

> IF THERE'S ANYTHING OUR KIDS NEED TODAY, IT'S THE SENSE OF SECURITY AND ACCEPTANCE THAT COMES FROM KNOWING THAT THEY ARE LOVED.

If there's anything our kids need today, it's the sense of security and acceptance that comes from knowing that they are loved. Children need to see Christianity being lived out in the home in a very authentic way with warmth, love, and laughter. When there is warm acceptance and love in the home, children won't run from Christianity. They'll embrace it, but when home is a place of strife, they'll often resist it.

Ken Anderson, president of Ken Anderson Films, says, "We have found that children go astray from homes where the solemn truths of the Bible are proclaimed as dynamic law, where parents, however sincere, fail to add that warmth of genuineness which must be seen for the Christian faith to ring real in a child's calculating mind." The way you behave at home, not only what you say, strongly influences your children. Let Jesus Christ, the Son of God, be your pattern to follow.

Did you know that Adolf Hitler heard the Word of God regularly as a young man? Even though he was instructed in the ways of God, because there was abuse in his home and a broken family situation, it caused bitterness to gain a stronghold which kept the Word of God from taking root down inside his heart.

He took over Germany in 1933 and ruled as a dictator until the end of World War II. During the years he was dictator, over 50,000,000 people would die as a result of the war; 6,000,000 of them were Jews. In killing the Jews, this is what he said: "By defending myself against the Jews, I am doing the Lord's work."

You see, when people get hardness of heart like that, they become wayside, pathway ground, and the enemy comes and snatches the Word, then they become deceived and believe a lie. You say, "Was Hitler lying?" Well, I sense that he was telling what he thought was the truth, but it happened because he was totally deceived. Once a person becomes hardened and the Word can't get in their heart they start believing lies instead of truth.

Certainly not all of Hitler's bad choices can be blamed on the breakdown in his home. However, if while young Adolf Hitler's mind was still pliable his home would have been a place where God's presence and peace had been felt instead of strife and abuse, surely it would have made a huge difference and quite possibly World War II and the Holocaust could have been prevented. What a thought!

Consider the following report by *The Journal of Research in Crime and Delinquency*. It states that the proportion of children from broken homes, particularly where the father is absent—regardless of socioeconomic or racial backgrounds—is the most reliable indicator of violent crime in that community. The report further states that most serious criminals were children who experienced abuse and neglect in early childhood.[6]

This is a pretty telling indicator of how important it is to gain control of our homes. Now, if you happen to be a single parent in a broken home situation, don't give in to despair. This is not about condemnation. There is hope. Our God specializes in making something beautiful out of broken things. You can still claim your home for God. If you are open, He is more than able to supernaturally step into your situation and help you turn your home into a haven of peace and empower you to raise champions for Him. The bottom line is this: Whether you are a two parent family or a single parent family, the home is a place that must be protected at all cost.

GOD SPECIALIZES IN MAKING SOMETHING BEAUTIFUL OUT OF BROKEN THINGS.

#2) The Church. Get your children and family in a church that's alive and the uncompromising Word of God is being taught with authority and is being lived out by the leaders. That means a church where people are being born again and lives are being changed. It's a church that's open to the power and moving of the Holy Spirit, where there's sound doctrine, genuine worship, prayer, evangelism, and real Christian relationships. All this is important to your young children and teenagers as they go through the growing process.

Also, as parents, to be truly effective you are going to need the gifts of the Spirit operating in your life for discernment and the word of wisdom and knowledge

---

[6]Douglas Smith & Roger Jarjoura, "Social Structure and Criminal Victimization," *Journal of Research in Crime and Delinquency 25*, February 1988.

to train your children. You need the gift of faith and the working of miracles. These aren't side issues—we need them. God's promises are given to us to reveal what God's will is for our lives and for our children's lives. These gifts come from the Holy Spirit to help us (1 Corinthians 12:1-10).

Sometimes parents just drop their kids off at church and think they are really helping their kids. And, dropping them off is better than not dropping them off, but if you want the maximum impact on your children, it's going to take family involvement, for both Mom and Dad to be there. I want to encourage you to get your kids in children's programs and teens in the youth programs.

Often parents will ask their kids if they want to go to children's church or youth groups. You know what? That's not the question to be asking. It's not a choice whether they're going to church or not—we're not voting. The statement to be made is, "We *are* going." So many parents have lost understanding of who's in charge of the home. They have inverted the authority and made the child the ruler. They live to cater to a little son or daughter's every whim. They want to keep their kids happy, happy all the time and not rock the boat. It's time for the parents to be the parents. Get your kids involved in church by participation. They may resist at first, but in the end, they'll respect you for it. It is simply a family commitment that we go together.

#3) The School. The school your children attend should reinforce what you believe on the key issues such as morality, homosexuality, abortion, alcohol and drugs, cursing, creation, truth, and inspiration of Scripture. In other words, if you are teaching one thing home, that's confirmed by the church, but is challenged by the educational system, then the child becomes confused. Who's telling the truth? Mom or my science teacher? Dad or my coach?

The following is a statement by well-known humanist leader Charles Potter. He said:

> Education is thus a most powerful ally of humanism, and every American school is a school of humanism. What can a theistic Sunday school's meeting for an hour once a week and teaching only a fraction of the children do to stem the tide of the five-day program of humanistic teaching?[7]

We must understand that where we are today in education is the result of deliberate plotting and planning from as far back as the early 1930's. For decades the humanists have been diligently pursuing the removal of God, prayer, the Bible, and morality, from our educational programs. While there are wonderful teachers within the public schools, there are certain leaders who have an agenda and they control the educational curriculum. We have seen evidence in books as early as kindergarten where same sex marriage and homosexuality are presented as lifestyles that are normal and should be accepted.

> WELL-KNOWN HUMANIST LEADER, CHARLES POTTER SAID, "EVERY AMERICAN SCHOOL IS A SCHOOL OF HUMANISM."

This agenda is not going to be something that is soft-sold. It's going to get harder and stronger. When

---

[7]Charles Francis Potter, *Humanism: A New Religion* (New York: Simon & Schuster, 1930), 3,128.

you see our media, you realize it is coming straight and center in TV, Internet, books and publications, movies, and in every direction. The humanist agenda is not just that we would accept them but that they plant their ungodly ideas into the hearts and minds of all the children in America. They understand, as we stated earlier in this book, that you change a culture by getting to its children. If children grow up seeing two men and a child presented as family in a public school textbook, they will just accept it and never challenge it.

You change a culture by getting to its children.

Take abortion for example. Today so many children accept abortion as okay because they were raised by an education system that never challenged it. If they are taught evolution, that we descended from monkeys, then that means an unborn child is just a fetus and not really a human being. You say, "How important is it?" It's the difference between life and death, whether a baby is murdered or whether you let the baby live. We are talking about major issues here that are going to get stronger and more serious. This is why we are very strong on homeschooling, Christian schooling, and parent involvement in other educational programs. We're talking about raising champions for God, that from the time they're in kindergarten all the way through twelfth grade, seven days a week—five days in school, two days in the home and church where they're getting consistent biblical training. The lack of consistent teaching is why so many of our young people in the hour we're living in are confused and disoriented on moral standards.

No matter what school your child is in, you need to get involved. Know what is being taught. Get right in the middle of the PTA and be involved with your teacher and principal and be a part of what's happening in that school. That's the only way it will work. We are grateful for the courageous superintendents, principals, coaches, and teachers in public schools who have taken a stand for the Lord.

BE A PART OF WHAT'S HAPPENING IN THAT SCHOOL.

#4) Friends. Because all children are looking for acceptance, their friends can have a significant influence on their lives. The right friends can build your child up, while the wrong ones can tear down what you are trying to establish in them. First Corinthians 15:33 NIV clearly states, *"Do not be misled: 'Bad company corrupts good character.'"* Make no mistake about it, the wrong company can corrupt, but the good news is, you have the authority over them and have the right to step in and monitor who your kids spend time with. God made you responsible for your children. You have the absolute responsibility and authority to make sure they are with the right kind of friends, friends who build up and compliment what you are doing at home.

This is the time for parents to shape up and get some backbone. You cannot raise champions unless you decide that you're in charge, that God made you responsible. You are driving the bus. The guy on the backseat is not directing you where to go. You've got a plan, a preassigned route you're going to take.

Now, obviously we can't control our children every minute of their lives. They are inevitably going to be with all types of people, but you can control what happens after school and evenings. Make an effort to see that they have friends who are like-minded, with similar standards and who have godly parents. The peer pressure that's put upon children is awesome. If your kids are around others who are using foul language or watching inappropriate movies, those words and images are getting into their minds. You've got to guard their minds from those situations. Listen to your children when they talk about their friends and you're going to know where those friends stand. You may need to tell your child that there are certain friends they are to love and witness to, but they're not going to spend time with them alone.

Teach your children to love everybody as Christ loves us, but you must also teach them to have discerning spirits regarding the types of friends they associate with. You must instill in them the courage to stand up for what's right even if they are with a circle of kids who are doing something wrong. By spending time with your child, training them in God's Word, you instill in them the character of Christ so they will be equipped to make the right decisions under pressure.

Once, one of our daughters heard some kids talking about buying a new pair of shoes and when they went to pay for them, the store clerk accidentally put the check into the shoe box rather than the cash drawer. The child said, "When we got home, we found the check so we just decided God wanted to bless us." Our daughter asked, "Mother, was that right? Would God do that?" Sharon said, "No, God wouldn't do that. God doesn't go against the principles of honesty that He has already established. That was wrong. That young girl went against her conscience, and if her mother keeps allowing her daughter to do that, then after a while things like that won't even bother her anymore."

#5) The Media. Radio, TV, Internet, iPod, cell phones, movies, books, magazines—this is an area where parents have got to absolutely draw the line because much of what you believe and stand for is opposed in the secular media. Proverbs 4:23 says, *"Keep* [guard] *your heart with all diligence, for out of it spring the issues of life."* Our eyes and ears are the gates to our heart so we must guard our gates with all diligence because what happens in our heart is going to direct our lives. If you don't guard the gates what gets into the heart will be corruption. Down through the years, we've watched parents who've said, "You know, we raised our children to love God. We prayed with them. We took them to church. We just don't know what happened." Two things I'll always ask: What were their friends like, and what type of media was going into their life?

> ✽
>
> WE MUST GUARD THE GATES TO OUR HEART WITH ALL DILIGENCE.
>
> ✽

We are living in a different day than people lived ten years ago. With the onslaught of the media, we have to make sure that our children are protected from ungodly influences. Just like all the other areas that we've talked about, you have a right to monitor TV, Radio, Internet, iPod, cell phone, and film content. You are still in charge. If your child or teenager has taken over your home then you need to pray, explain what needs to happen to your family, and reestablish parental authority in the home.

> ✽
>
> IF YOUR CHILD OR TEENAGER HAS TAKEN OVER YOUR HOME THEN YOU NEED TO PRAY AND REESTABLISH PARENTAL AUTHORITY IN THE HOME.
>
> ✽

We as parents have jurisdiction from an oversight standpoint; other families can't come in and rip your children out of your home because you have legal custody over them. You are charged with establishing a safe environment and boundary lines for your children's protection and security. I've had people say, "You mean you don't let your kids go out of control?" I say, "No. We are in charge." That's it. It's very simple. My son John just recently commented on this very thing in an interview he did. Listen to what he said.

Our parents were very careful what they let come before our eyes growing up. Whatever movie came out we were not allowed to watch it until my parents had checked on it first. I remember us being in theaters with our family watching a movie and some situation came up and my dad said, "All right, we're leaving," and he would make us get up and walk out of the theater. And, you know, a lot of kids made fun of us. They were like, "You guys aren't allowed to watch the Simpsons?" Not to bash on that cartoon, because some people watch it. I'm not saying you're a sinner if you watch that, but just certain things and certain shows like the Simpsons promote unbiblical ideals. My parents saw that there was a rebellious attitude in that TV show, and they were like, "We don't want that getting inside our kids." Sometimes we were upset, but they would always explain. They would say, "Now, this is why we don't watch this."

I remember there was one show we were watching and the daughter was yelling at her father and my parents said, "See this girl who's yelling at her father? The Daughertys don't do this." And they would always explain why. They wouldn't just say, "No movies." They would always explain why and that helped. I mean, we were still bummed that we couldn't watch it, but it helped because we were like, "Okay, at least we know why."

There are a lot of great things that are out there in the media. I'm not talking about shutting it all down. I'm talking about filtering what's coming in to your family. In order to raise champion children we must be watchmen and guard the media that comes into our homes and we must guard what goes in front of our children's eyes and ears to screen what they get and what they don't get. If they are not getting what the rest of their friends are getting, God will find a way to make it up to them. You must guard your children's lives.

Our daughter Sarah said, *"As I look back, I appreciate that my parents guarded what we watched, and listened to; it really helped me stay pure in so many ways."*

FAITH IN ACTION

Again, spend some time in prayer and reflection about this chapter. Ask God to reveal to you any of the five critical areas of influence of which you may need to get control. Write down those areas and then pray over them. As you pray, listen for the Holy Spirit's insight and revelation. Write that down as well. Remember, you're the parent. You have the power to make the right choices for your children.

Areas I Need to Get Control

1._____

2._____

3._____

4._____

5._____

"For I will pour water on him who is thirsty, and floods on the dry ground; I will pour My Spirit on your descendants, and My blessing on your offspring" Isaiah 44:3.

"But thus says the Lord: 'Even the captives of the mighty shall be taken away, and the prey of the terrible be delivered; for I will contend with him who contends with you, and I will save your children'" Isaiah 49:25.

6

FIRST COMMAND OBEDIENCE

*"If you are willing and obedient, you shall eat
the good of the land; but if you refuse and rebel,
you shall be devoured by the sword...."*
— **Isaiah 1:19-20**

Certainly, most parents desire to have happy, well-adjusted, successful kids who honor God. Yet, when raising champions for the Lord, there is a higher goal. Our ultimate goal is to have kids who will obey God and do His will. And not *just* that they obey God, but that they obey at His first command. There's an old adage that says, "Slow obedience is no obedience." It's true. First command obedience is critical to being a champion for God and experiencing His absolute best. Being slow to obey or not obeying God can have serious conse-

> ❧
>
> FIRST COMMAND
> OBEDIENCE IS CRITICAL
> TO BEING A CHAMPION
> FOR GOD.
>
> ❧

quences for our children. They could miss God's best purpose for their lives, or worse, end up in destructive lifestyles.

Bill Myers' Obedience to God

Bill Myers' story is an example of what can happen when our kids have been trained to obey God. Bill has impacted the world as the best-selling author of hundreds of Christian books for children and teens. He's also the creator/producer of numerous Christian films. He created and produced the wildly successful children's series *McGee and Me* which has instilled godly values into millions of kids around the world. Bill's ministry is not the result of his own personal dream, but of obedience to God's first command.

Growing up, Bill was taught that Jesus needed to be at the foundation of everything he did and that it was important to *"never say 'no' to God."* Also growing up, his parents had protected him from viewing anything ungodly that went against their standards. Bill's parents only allowed him to watch wholesome shows like *Mary Poppins, Swiss Family Robinson,* etc. When he was a freshman in college, he had his sights set on becoming a dentist. It seemed like a respectable, mature type profession upon which to aspire, but God had other plans.

One night Bill was with some of the guys in the dorm and they watched the movie *The Godfather.* His friends acted like it was no big deal. They had been desensitized, but Bill was shocked. He'd never seen anything like it. *"I wandered around the campus for several days, numb,"* Bill said. As he walked, he began a dialogue with God. *"God, You've got to raise people up in communications. Film is so powerful, and look how it's being used!"*

A resonating impression nagged at him that he had come to recognize down through the years as God's voice. *"Come on, get serious,"* he continued. *"I'm saying You've got to raise up people who are film directors and people in communications to combat this stuff . . . Not me, God! I don't know anything about film."* But the impression kept building and building, until Bill says, *"It became real clear God wanted me to be a part of what I was praying for."*

Bill didn't hesitate. He immediately sought to change his major to film directing. One problem, though: The university he was attending didn't have a film directing department. So, out of faith and obedience, Bill transferred to a small college, the only one he could find in his area that had a film department. That was the first of many obedient steps that would eventually lead him to a ministry impacting the whole world. Thank God for Bill's obedience and thank God for his parents who were not afraid or ashamed to enforce godly standards!

Bill's story is a powerful illustration of what God can do in our kids' lives when they learn to obey Him at His first command. This is why discipline and training are so important. If your children can't obey you now, someone whom they *can* see, how will they later obey God's Holy Spirit whom they *can't* see? If they can't obey your rules now, how will they be able to obey the Word of God later? You prepare your children to honor and obey God by training and disciplining them to honor and obey *your* words.

Training for First Command Obedience

Training for first command obedience is really quite simple. Speak clearly and precisely what is to be done <u>one</u> time. Just once, that's it. "Johnny, sit down." It's clear. It's precise. It's calm. If little Johnny doesn't obey on the first command, then he needs correction and discipline. Here's the thing: If you have to repeat what you want several times, raising your voice each time, then you are actually training your child to know what decibel level means action on your part. Don't fool yourself. Kids know exactly at what decibel level they must obey. A child can be trained to obey after the third time they are told, the tenth time, or to obey after the first time. It all depends on the trainer. Your children will be disciplined upon the basis of your level of tolerance or intolerance. They will rise to a higher standard or fall to a lower standard depending on where you set it.

> ❧
>
> KIDS KNOW EXACTLY AT WHAT DECIBEL LEVEL THEY MUST OBEY.
>
> ❧

Think about it. How soon do you want your children to obey God? After He tells them for five years to do something? What if Bill Myers had not obeyed God or was slow in obeying and wandered around for several years debating about it? Think of the time that would have been lost. Many times what God wants to accomplish is based on His perfect timing. When a person disobeys, they often miss God's timing and He is forced to find someone else who *will* obey. So, your responsibility as a parent raising champion children is to train them to obey on your first command, not after multiple warnings.

In addition to helping them experience God's best, first command obedience can also protect our children from harm. It can literally save their lives. When Sarah was two years old, first command obedience saved her life. One day, she was looking out of the sliding glass door and saw a little kitty cat in the yard across the street. Unbeknown to us, she pushed open the door and took off running towards it. At the same time, a car was speeding down the street. Sarah, of course, had no comprehension of the approaching car and the driver of the car didn't see her. Thank the Lord a neighbor from across the street had stepped out of her front door just as Sarah was coming to the edge of the street. After seeing what was going on, the neighbor shouted at the top of her lungs, "Sarah! Stop!" Immediately Sarah froze still in her tracks at the curb precisely as the car went flying by. Because of her instant obedience Sarah's life was spared.

ॐ

FIRST COMMAND OBEDIENCE CAN ALSO PROTECT OUR CHILDREN FROM HARM. IT CAN LITERALLY SAVE THEIR LIVES.

ॐ

Years ago, I was in a deep conversation with a twenty-two-year-old young man about the importance of not just hearing the Word of God but of being a doer of the Word and of being obedient to God and the blessings that come from it. "You know," he said, "growing up, my parents never made me do anything. I just did what I wanted. I've never had to obey anyone. Whatever I felt I wanted to do, that's what I did. I can't really understand obeying God's Word."

As he was talking, it suddenly hit me how critical training a child to instantly obey their parents really is. A child who has been taught instant obedience to his parents will usually exercise instant obedience to

69

God's Word when they begin to hear it. In doing so, they will be delivered from hell and many other destructive consequences. They'll understand the penalty for disobedience and then the blessing for obedience.

In the chapters to come we will learn how to actually implement the training and discipline of your champions.

FAITH IN ACTION

Spend time in prayer asking the Lord for the understanding and importance of first command obedience. Ask Him to help you to be calm, clear, firm, and consistent so your children will not be confused. Try to bring to mind instances in your own life where past obedience has been critical. Write down any insights and revelations that the Holy Spirit brings to your mind.

Insights and Revelations

_____

_____

_____

_____

_____

"All your children shall be taught by the Lord, and great shall be the peace of your children" Isaiah 54:13.

"For I have known him, in order that he may command his children and his household after him, that they keep the way of the Lord, to do righteousness and justice, that the Lord may bring to Abraham what He has spoken to him" Genesis 18:19.

"Children, obey your parents in the Lord, for this is right" Ephesians 6:1.

7

SOLDIERS ARE TRAINED NOT JUST TAUGHT

"Train up a child in the way he should go, and when he is old he will not depart from it."
— Proverbs 22:6

If we are going to raise champions to walk in obedience to God, then we need to take a closer look at the above scripture. Many parents quote this verse and then get discouraged when their children become rebellious and even walk away from the things of God. They throw up their hands in defeat believing it doesn't work for them. On the surface, it appears that God has not kept His promise. But what we must understand is that there is a big, important difference between training and teaching and most parents confuse the

THE DIFFERENCE BETWEEN TEACHING AND TRAINING IS SO SIGNIFICANT THAT NOT RECOGNIZING IT CAN CAUSE A FUNDAMENTAL BREAKDOWN IN THE PARENTING PROCESS.

two. They think they are training when, in fact, they are actually only teaching or instructing which is not nearly as effective. Training our children is what God has called us to do. The difference is so significant that not recognizing it can cause a fundamental breakdown in the parenting process. So, what *is* the difference?

Training vs. Teaching

Training is a military term that has to do with *making* a person do a requested task. *Webster's* says "to train" is "to form by instruction, exercise, discipline, or drill; to make prepared for a test of skill." Training involves instruction, explanation, demonstration, and then hands-on repetition until the task is done the right way.

Whenever a recruit joins the military and goes through boot camp, then on to the base camp to learn their assigned specialty, it's not called military teaching. It's called military training. Soldiers get trained not taught. Now, there is some classroom teaching involved, but then they go out into the field and actually do hands-on implementation of what they were shown. In the training process, the soldiers are not only told what to do, but are shown by example what to do. Then, they do it themselves. When it's not done right the first time, they are corrected and do it again and again for as long as it takes to get it right.

With each do-over they get a little more instruction on the things they need to improve on. As time passes they get more and more proficient. Through this training process an awesome transformation takes place. Average Joe recruit is turned from an out-of-shape, sometimes rebellious, eighteen year old, into a lean, fully obedient soldier prepared for battle. That's the

difference between merely teaching and training.
Training sets clear goals, gives
solid instructions, makes firm
demands, and then enforces
them.

You train up a child in the
way they should go. Like a soldier in the military, you make
them do it right again and again
until it becomes ingrained in
them and then, when they get
older, they will not depart from it. That's a huge difference than someone saying, "Well, I've told those
kids a thousand times what was the right thing to do
and they just don't listen." No. That's not what God
said to do. He said to *train* them not just *tell* them.
Training is making them do the right thing, with the
right attitude, as many times as it takes until they get
it. A subtle lie has crept into many families today in
the discipline area that says, *"Don't ever make children
do anything they don't want to do. You might damage
their self-esteem."*

Well, I'm sure there are a lot of things that children
and young people may not like to do, but just because
they don't like to do them doesn't mean we are not supposed to make them do it. And by "make" I mean
"make." All children, including those cute little curly
headed, sparkly eyed, precious children, are born with
indwelling human natures and not knowing right from
wrong. Therefore, if you let them choose for themselves, they are certain to choose wrong. I'm praying
for a strengthening of backbone in moms and dads to
make their children do what's right.

> ❧
>
> TRAINING SETS CLEAR
> GOALS, GIVES SOLID
> INSTRUCTIONS, MAKES
> FIRM DEMANDS, AND
> THEN ENFORCES THEM.
>
> ❧

75

Over the past several years there has developed a spirit of rebellion which has allowed children to rule and dominate their parents, to make them bow to what the kids want. But God commands us as parents to train our children and that means not only teaching and telling them, but showing them and leading them through what we want them to do, and then making them do it.

Now, I know all of this may sound hard and tough on both the children and the parents. And I'm not advocating running your home like the military where there is no fun or freedom. But remember, even when they resist, children actually experience more peace and freedom when there are clear rules and distinct boundaries. Even so, sometimes it will be tough on them and you'll have to make some hard choices. You've heard the saying "tough love." When we truly love our children there will be times that we'll have to be tough on them.

Properly Trained for the Front Lines

Training means you are willing to do whatever it takes to go through the process again and again. "How many times are we going to have to tear this rifle apart and put it together?" a drill sergeant questions his recruit. He knows it doesn't mean anything until that recruit is in the heat of battle and needs to do it in the dark. As a parent raising champions, you've got to realize that your children are going to face the enemy and demonic spirits and if they are not trained and prepared and strong for it, they are going to be overwhelmed and defeated. Get the understanding of a drill sergeant. He may be acting tough, but it's only because he understands that his eighteen-year-old recruit is one day going to be out on the front lines with his life and the lives of his unit at stake. If that recruit is not properly trained, lives are going to be lost. A drill sergeant starts with the end in mind and so must you. If you don't have this mind-set, the way you'll approach the parenting process is going to be something like, "Well, I just want to do whatever makes them happy, or I just hate to see them disappointed, or I hate conflict and just want peace in the house." Why not do what makes them strong, because the peaceable fruit of righteousness and obedience will be the end result.

Stormie Omartian's Story of Tough Love

Author Stormie Omartian tells the following story in her best-selling book *The Power of a Praying Parent.* It's a powerful example of a parent's tough love in action when training a child, or in this particular account, a teenager.

When my son was fourteen years old, he covered his bedroom walls with posters of the musicians he admired most. The problem was that in some of the pictures both the attire and the music being represented were offensive to his father and me and not glorifying to God. When we asked Christopher to take those particular posters down and explained why, he balked, then with a less than humble spirit did what we asked. A short time later, however, he replaced them with new ones which were just as bad. We again confronted him, took appropriate disciplinary measures, and this time we took them all down for him.

Christopher was not happy, and we recognized we were dealing with the early manifestations of a rebellious spirit. So we decided to do as the Bible says and "put on the whole armor of God that you may be able to stand against the wiles of the devil" (Ephesians 6:11). We prayed, we employed the Word of God, and we professed our faith in God's ability to make us overcomers. We did battle in the Spirit and witnessed the peace of God take control of the situation. Our son's attitude changed, and the next time he put up posters they met the requirements we, as his parents, had established. This was the power of God in action, employed by praying parents.

Wall posters seem like such a minor issue now, but at the time we were dealing with a strong will that was exalting itself over parents and God. And by resisting that display of rebellion, we were able to stop it before it became something major. We were determined to win the struggle because we knew we had God and His Word on our side and because for our son, something eternal was at stake.[8]

Yes, when training up a child in the ways of the Lord it's sometimes going to require that tough, strong attitude. But that's okay because we're training soldiers for God's army. Champions.

---

[8]Stormie Omartian, *The Power of a Praying Parent* (Eugene, OR: Harvest House, 1995), 61.

FAITH IN ACTION

Ask God to grant you the wisdom to know when you need to be compassionate and gentle and when you need to be tough like a military drill sergeant. Ask Him to help you to see that sometimes being loving requires that you be tough because you are training your children for the battle of life.

Write down areas you feel weak in and need improvement. Mix faith with the sword of God's Word. Believe that God is pouring His Spirit and blessings out upon you and your children.

Areas of Training Where I Need Improvement

1)_____

2)_____

3)_____

4)_____

5)_____

"For the word of God is living and powerful, and sharper than any two-edged sword, piercing even to the division of soul and spirit, and of joints and marrow, and is a discerner of the thoughts and intents of the heart" Hebrews 4:12.

"The secret things belong to the Lord our God, but those things which are revealed belong to us and to our children forever, that we may do all the words of this law" Deuteronomy 29:29.

8

GODLY CORRECTION
AND PEACEABLE FRUIT

"'My son, do not despise the chastening of the Lord, nor be discouraged when you are rebuked by Him; for whom the Lord loves He chastens, and scourges every son whom He receives.' If you endure chastening, God deals with you as with sons; for what son is there whom a father does not chasten? But if you are without chastening, of which all have become partakers, then you are illegitimate and not sons. Furthermore, we have had human fathers who corrected us, and we paid them respect. Shall we not much more readily be in subjection to the Father of spirits and live? For they indeed for a few days chastened us as seemed best to them, but He for our profit, that we may be partakers of His holiness. Now no chastening seems to be joyful for the present, but painful; nevertheless, afterward it yields the peaceable fruit of righteousness to those who have been trained by it."

— Hebrews 12:5-11

Even though the above passage is a bit long, I felt it was important for you to read it in order to get its full impact. Basically, it's saying that God loves us and one of the ways He shows that love is to chastise or discipline us. The word "chastening" in this passage is also translated as "correction" or "discipline." Wherever you see it, you can insert one of those two words. The way we know that God loves us is that He disciplines us. He does so because He knows that eventually it will produce in us the peaceable fruits of holiness—His character. Godly discipline therefore is a sign, not that God is mad at us, but that we are His children and He loves us.

Never experiencing God's discipline is a sign that we are *not* His. Have you ever wondered how some people in the world can get away with certain behaviors and actions? It's because they don't belong to God and they just do whatever they want, even if it ends up with their own destruction. When you become a child of God, a higher standard is applied to your life. You're not saved because of that standard but because of His amazing grace. Then, because you have become the righteousness of God by faith, you are now called to live like it. When you become a child of God, He begins the process of forming His character in you and part of that forming process involves discipline.

THE MOST LOVING THING YOU WILL EVER DO FOR YOUR CHILDREN IS TO DISCIPLINE THEM.

To Love Is to Discipline

Perhaps the *most* loving thing you will ever do for your children is to discipline them. Like God does with us, our reason for disciplining our children is because we love them and desire to see godly character developed in them. The goal in discipline and correction should always be character development: training our children in the principles of godly character. It's the lessons of discipline that will ultimately yield the peaceable fruit of righteousness and holiness in them.

As a parent, you can do all the other things we've talked about in this book, and they are good, important things, but if you fail to discipline you will be letting your kids down in a very serious way. Godly discipline is a part of the glue that holds all the other principles together.

Cultivating the peaceable fruit of righteousness into the hearts of our children begins with establishing the fear of the Lord. We're living in a society today that, for the most part, doesn't have a reverential fear of God. Many things are done without a sense of reprisal or judgment. There's no sense of honor, holiness, or integrity. As a result, lives are wrecked because the wages of sin is death, not only in eternity, but here and now. Sin extracts a high penalty right here on the earth. People are being destroyed because they don't fear God. The fear of the Lord is to depart from evil. It's the beginning of wisdom and this must be instilled in our children through discipline.

Our children must be taught to respect authority. They must be taught hard work, responsibility, faithfulness, integrity, and honesty, as opposed to stealing, cheating, and lying; and that there are negative consequences to wrong behavior. When you discipline without instilling godly principles into your children's lives, they may not even know why they are being corrected. This is why you have to be very clear and firm when disciplining.

Correction vs. Punishment

Frustration exists when the rules aren't clearly defined and consistently enforced. Let me encourage you to use the word "correction" rather than "punishment." The purpose of correction is to alter the course of a child's life. It involves self-control, love, instruction, reproof, repentance, and affirmation.

Proverbs 29:15 KJV says, *"The rod and reproof give wisdom, but a child left to himself bringeth his mother to shame."* Some people give the rod, but they don't give the reproof. Therefore, wisdom doesn't come into the child. You must correct with the rod, but you must also correct by sowing the Word of God in the heart.

The key to discipline and correction is your spirit. If you punish with hostility, anger, frustration, or in some cases even hatred, you'll input those same forces inside the child's heart. They'll pick up the spirit as much as they pick up what they feel in the natural!

Not only are your children being trained, but you, as a parent, are being trained. If you're training your children not to lose their temper, then don't lose yours while you're correcting them. You train, not only by what you say, but by what you communicate through your spirit, your words, and your gestures.

Now, the act of applying correction and discipline is never a pleasant process for the child or for the parents. It doesn't always *feel* like the peaceable fruit of righteousness is being formed in them. Remember though, we don't go by our feelings but by the Word of God, and the Word says that the process of discipline will produce the peaceable fruit of righteousness in them. So, while going through the arduous process of discipline, keep confessing in your mind, "Lord, I'm believing You for the peaceable fruits of righteousness that are coming after this. I am standing on Your Word that they are going to be partakers of Your holiness because we are paying the price for it right now. God, thank You for honoring Your promises."

Discipline with Kindness and Gentleness

Even though the discipline process can get extremely trying at times, it should always be done out of kindness and gentleness, never anger. It's important that you get control of yourself before you take any disciplinary action. Pray and ask for God's help. Give yourself some time to cool down and think.

> ॐ
>
> IT'S IMPORTANT THAT YOU GET CONTROL OF YOURSELF BEFORE YOU TAKE ANY DISCIPLINARY ACTION.
>
> ॐ

When one of our kids did something wrong, Sharon or I would say, "Okay, you sit down in your room. I'll be back in just a few minutes." Then, we'd leave the room. Why? To get control of ourselves and give the process time, to let the child sit, to prepare ourselves to have a loving attitude with no anger. Remember, if you discipline in anger, you drive anger into the child.

Anger and screaming at a child don't produce the fruit of righteousness. What they do is transfer the spirit of anger that's inside of you into them. That's why it's so important for you to take some time to regroup. Do whatever it takes to get in control. "Lord, help me." Pray in the Holy Spirit. "Lord, help me keep control of myself and respond in love."

Discipline Promptly

Proverbs 13:24 says, *"He who spares his rod hates his son, but he who loves him disciplines him promptly."* The word "promptly" is translated here as early or quickly. In other words, you apply it according to when the need is. Notice, the verse also says, *"He who spares his rod hates his son."*

According to the Word of God, not only do you love your child if you discipline them, you hate them if you don't. You hate your child. That is pretty heavy. How many of you remember your mom and dad saying, "I'm doing this because I love you"? Now you have the verse for it. That's what I would do. I'd tell them, "I love you and the Bible says for me to discipline you."

The type of "rod" we used for the discipline process was a little wooden spoon. It wasn't harmful or dangerous, but it had sufficient enough administrative pain to make an influence. We called it "The Board of Education" applied to the "Seat of Knowledge." Now, I want to say this about discipline; you are going to get to certain ages with older children where you move from the rod to withholding privileges.

There are many types of ways parents can utilize withholding opportunities which can be quite painful for teenagers. A simple example is, all their friends may be getting to go somewhere, doing some fun activity, but the child being disciplined may have to stay home in their room. That is often more painful than getting spanked.

When giving godly discipline, it's important that the child has an opportunity to say what they did wrong and then repent to God and you. Come back in the room and ask them, "Okay, Johnny, do you know why I am disciplining you?" If they don't know, then calmly explain it to them. Afterwards ask them, "Now, are you ready to repent?" and you teach them how to repent and what it means, first to God and second, repenting to the one they have offended.

Discipline in the Love of God

The next step is to administer the discipline in the love of God. Then, hug and affirm them. Tell them how great they are. "I believe in you. You're a champion for God." You can act in love because you're under control. You're not screaming and yelling because you're not angry, they're not getting angry, and they understand that the rod was about correction.

Proverbs 29:15 says, *"The rod and rebuke give wisdom, but a child left to himself brings shame to his mother."* Parents raising champions understand that instead of leaving their children to do whatever they want to do, they are going to give the rod and rebuke. In other words, they are going to explain to their children the reason for the discipline action. It's very important that you as a parent grasp how you are instructing your child for spiritual response to God. The rod with reproof is so important because it's the truth that sets people free.

Second Timothy 3:15-17 says, *"And that from childhood you have known the Holy Scriptures, which are able to make you wise for salvation through faith which is in Christ Jesus. All Scripture is given by inspiration of God, and is profitable for doctrine, for reproof, for correction, for instruction in righteousness, that the man of God may be complete, thoroughly equipped for every good work."* Notice, the Apostle Paul went back to Timothy's childhood, to the Word of God that was

put in him. So, when you are administering godly discipline, you are putting the Word of God inside of
them.

Discipline:
The Stronger-willed Parent

You say, "But I have a strong-willed child." Then,
you need to be a stronger-willed parent. Your will has
the ability to be stronger than
your child's will. It's great to
have a strong-willed child. You
just need to have a stronger
will—that they understand you
are going to have the will of God
done in your house, not the will
of rebellion. Make up your mind
to do whatever it takes to please God. The discipline and
correction we are defining are not to be brutal, dangerous, damaging, or cruel. It is to be done in love, with
gentleness, yet strong enough to get their attention and
help them decide to correct wrong behavior.

> ~
>
> YOU SAY, "BUT I HAVE A
> STRONG-WILLED CHILD."
> THEN, YOU NEED TO BE A
> STRONGER-WILLED PARENT.
>
> ~

Discipline While There Is Hope

Proverbs 19:18 KJV says, *"Chasten thy son while
there is hope, and let not thy soul spare for his crying."*
How many times does a parent stop the discipline
process because a kid is crying? Surely, when you spank
their bottom they're going to cry! That's what happens
when you correct children. Get over them controlling
and manipulating you with their tears (teenagers can
still pull this). *". . . let not thy soul spare for his crying."*
And *"Chasten while there is hope."* There is a season
when children are going to respond to discipline. You
need to deal with them while there is hope in their lives.
Crying shouldn't change our response to discipline.

Many children control and train their parents rather than their parents training them. If you have set a pattern and a standard for raising a champion for God, then you are the one in charge of bringing them up and training them to that point.

Proverbs 22:15 says, *"Foolishness is bound up in the heart of a child; the rod of correction will drive it far from him."* You have to explain to the child being disciplined that what they did was rebellion and that it was disobedience and disobedience is sin. <u>Consider what the child is going to be like in your home when they reach the ages of thirteen to seventeen if foolishness and rebellion are still in them.</u>

I'll never forget when I was a young boy being in the home of a friend when his high school brother walked through the house. We were having a Cub Scout meeting and that boy cursed his mother out in front of all the Cub Scouts. He kicked over things and slammed the door. I'd never seen anything like it and it frightened me. In that home, that young man had never been properly controlled. Then, when he hit a certain age, he was out of control. Eventually that young man went to prison. I'm speaking to you parents who think, *We'll just kind of let them get away with what they want.* Rebellion and disobedience may be cute when they are four or five, but just wait until they are sixteen and can drive their fist through the door!

Proverbs 23:13-14 NIV says, *"Do not withhold discipline from a child; if you punish him with the rod, he will not die. Punish him with the rod and save his soul from death."* Listen, if you discipline your child with the rod, they will not die. Now, they may think they are going to die. You just say to them, "You're not going to die, Honey."

"... *save his soul from death.*" Other translations say hell and eternal death. Listen to me. The discipline of children has eternal consequences. If it's done in the right way, at the right time, it can prepare a child to obey God and be saved. It can also save their lives from ruin in this life. Otherwise, the lack of discipline or wrong discipline can destroy that child's life.

I'm reminded of a young man from our city whom we didn't meet until he was in Oklahoma's McAlester Prison on death row. When Sharon and I went there to minister, I asked him his name and where he was from. He said, "Tulsa." He recognized our name and said, "I used to ride a bus to a certain church in Tulsa." So, this young man knew the Lord. He loved God, but started running with a group of young men who were on the wrong track. I asked him what happened, and he said, "Mama told me not to hang out with those guys, but I didn't obey."

Well, the day came when that group robbed a store. A gun was shot and someone was killed. He's in prison today for it. His destiny was destroyed because of disobedience and wrong associations. Now, in this case, the young man made his own choice to disobey. Who knows what could have been diverted if proper discipline was administered and godly character was planted into him when he was younger? We will never know. My friend, the discipline of your children is very serious business not to be taken lightly.

> ~
>
> IF YOU OVERTHROW THE AUTHORITY OF A LEADER WHO IS IN THEIR LIFE, THEN YOU WILL BE UNDERMINING YOUR OWN AUTHORITY.
>
> ~

If one of our kids had a problem at school, we didn't call up the school and say, "Hey, I don't agree with what you've done." We stood with the school officials. If there was a problem at school, then we disciplined them at home just like they disciplined them at school. If you overthrow the authority of a leader who is in their life, then you will be undermining your own authority.

Discipline Consistently

Another thing that's important to know when disciplining is to be consistent and persistent. Stay with it even when you don't want to do it. It will pay off in the long run. You see, the enemy's tactic against discipline is to weary you and wear you down and cause you to take what appears to be an easy path of non-discipline or partial discipline. Every parent faces the issue of being tired. If the enemy can get you to back off, then foolishness and rebellion can gain a stronghold. And that's the enemy's goal. Keep the vision and the vision will keep you as you are raising champions for God.

Follow Discipline with
Affirmation and Encouragement

Finally, the last part of godly discipline is affirmation and encouragement. Declare into your child from start to finish what you believe about them. "You're a child of God. You're a champion. You are blessed and redeemed. You're delivered, victorious, and peaceful." There are so many things that need to be said. Mainly, they need to hear and know that you believe in them, that you love them. You see, wrong action doesn't make a bad child. Just because a child threw something or hit someone or did something wrong doesn't mean they're bad. You simply correct

> DECLARE INTO YOUR CHILD FROM START TO FINISH WHAT YOU BELIEVE ABOUT THEM.

the behavior and bring them back to the truth of who they are in Christ. They're a champion for the Lord.

Hugging and encouraging after discipline are so important. Children want to know after discipline that you still love them, that you believe in them. After discipline is a good time to spend some extra time doing what they like. Go get some ice cream with them. Do something fun with them so they understand the act of discipline has not separated you from them.

> ❧
>
> DO SOMETHING FUN
> WITH THEM SO THEY
> UNDERSTAND THE ACT
> OF DISCIPLINE HAS NOT
> SEPARATED YOU
> FROM THEM.
>
> ❧

What's important at that point is for parents to leave it and move on. Romans 8:1 says, *"There is therefore now no condemnation. . . ."* Once the issue is dealt with, we are leaving it behind. We are not going to hold guilt and shame over them. We've forgiven them. If it happens again, then simply repeat the process over.

- This is what we said—what the standard is;

- This is what you did—what they did wrong;

- This is what we told you would happen—the consequences.

Reinforce the Positive

Don't forget to reinforce the positive in the midst of maintaining discipline. An effective part of character development in children is the reinforcement of the positives in their lives. Many parents, with an appropriate motive of correcting and bringing proper training, get off course by faultfinding rather than accentuating the positives.

Perfectionism will cause bitterness in children, because children aren't perfect. If you could see a video of how you acted when you were growing up, it might help your memory! Raising champion children involves finding reasons to praise them in what they are doing right in their lives. Today, many kids are under oppression because they have a barrage of accusations against them day in and day out. You can change that by speaking that which is good over them. As the old song says, "Accentuate the positive, eliminate the negative, latch on to the affirmative, and don't mess with Mr. In-between!" This doesn't mean you don't deal with the negatives. It's just that you focus on the good in each of your children and make something out of it. Let praise come from your lips to your children.

> ❧
>
> RAISING CHAMPION CHILDREN INVOLVES FINDING REASONS TO PRAISE THEM IN WHAT THEY ARE DOING RIGHT IN THEIR LIVES.
>
> ❧

Mark 10:13-16 says, *"Then they brought young children to Him [Jesus], that He might touch them; but the disciples rebuked those who brought them. But when Jesus saw it, He was greatly displeased and said to them, 'Let the little children come to Me, and do not forbid them; for of such is the kingdom of God. Assuredly, I say to you, whoever does not receive the kingdom of God as a little child will by no means enter it.' And He took them up in His arms, laid His hands on them, and blessed them."*

When was the last time you took your children in your arms and blessed them in the power of the Holy

Spirit? When is the last time you really hugged your teenager and told them how special they were? We need to touch our children and bless them just as Jesus took them up in His arms and blessed them.

A large youth group was asked the question, "How many of you have had your mother or father hug you and tell you 'I love you' in the last week? Over 50 percent of the teenagers present said they hadn't been hugged or told they were loved during the previous week. It's okay to hug teenagers! It's okay to hug little children and take them in your arms and love them! If there's anything young people need today, it's the sense of security and acceptance that comes from knowing that they are loved. Jesus wasn't uptight with little children, and neither should we! Regardless of their age, accentuate the positive and bless your children.

As parents raising champions, if we follow these steps in discipline and trust God, we can be assured that godly character will be planted deep into the souls of our children and one day will produce a harvest of peaceable righteousness in their lives.

FAITH IN ACTION

Pray for courage: Lord, grant me the courage to discipline. Help me to trust in You and to know that though it may be unpleasant now, it will produce the peaceable fruit of righteousness in my child and may ultimately save their life. Help me not to be manipulated by their crying and pleading, but to stand firm in my conviction. And Lord, help me to always discipline in love and to affirm them afterwards. Thank You, Lord, for Your promises.

Areas Where My Children Need Discipline

1)_____

2)_____

3)_____

4)_____

5)_____

"Don't hesitate to discipline children. A good spanking won't kill them. As a matter of fact, it may save their lives" Proverbs 23:13-14 TEV.

"Correct your son, and he will give you rest; yes, he will give delight to your soul" Proverbs 29:17.

"I have been young, and now am old; yet I have not seen the righteous forsaken, nor his descendants begging bread" Psalm 37:25.

"He himself shall dwell in prosperity, and his descendants shall inherit the earth" Psalm 25:13.

THE MOST VALUABLE GIFT

"For this reason a man will leave his father and mother and be united to his wife, and the two will become one flesh."
— *Matthew 19:5* NIV

Outside of leading them to Jesus, a strong, loving marriage is the most valuable gift you will ever give to your children. A child's most basic sense of well-being comes from knowing that their parents love each other. It brings comfort and reassurance to their lives. A strong marriage creates a strong household and a strong household produces confident, godly children. Therefore, if we are going to raise champions for God it means being intentional about building a strong and loving marriage. It means not just being married, but becoming one.

If your marriage is weak, your children will pick up on it. They will feel it. When spouses constantly argue and bicker, and are seldom or never affectionate, children will learn to behave this way. On the flip side, however, if your marriage is affectionate and loving, then boys will learn how to properly treat women and girls will learn how to bless their future husbands. Children have an amazing ability to sense when things are wrong and when things are right.

It's vital that, as a parent, you demonstrate the ability to work through problems with your spouse in an understanding and grace oriented way. In addition, if you are not both on the same page as parents, your discipline will become contradictory and confusing to your children. However, couples who are <u>one</u> in their marriage relationship are more likely to agree on their disciplinary practices. This provides consistent expectations to the children. When Christian parents model positive love and show honor to each other, it goes a long way towards validating their parental teachings.

Having a strong, loving marriage relationship should be a priority in your life because it not only gives personal satisfaction, but it creates an atmosphere that your children will want to be a part of and emulate. Do whatever it takes to strengthen and protect your marriage relationship.

&

IT'S CRITICAL TO REMEMBER THAT THE FOUNDATION FOR THE PARENTING ROLE IS A STRONG MARRIAGE PARTNERSHIP.

&

The Power of Unity

Now, we all know that strong marriages don't just happen. They require a significant investment of time and energy. And while there is a need to balance the role of spouse with the role of parent, it's critical to remember that the foundation for the parenting role is a strong marriage partnership. The marriage comes first.

You see, when you are <u>one</u> with your spouse, your power is duplicated. God's power is multiplied in the marriage relationship, particularly when you walk in agreement and in harmony with each other. In Matthew 18:19-20 AMP the Lord says:

Again I tell you, if two of you on earth agree (harmonize together, together make a symphony) about—anything and everything—whatever they shall ask, it will come to pass and be done for them by My Father in heaven.

For wherever two or three are gathered (drawn together as My followers) in (into) My name, there I AM in the midst of them.

That's not just a mental agreement. It's not just physically touching and saying, "I agree with you." The real power is in spiritual agreement where two people are in harmony in their spirits. There's no greater potential of power of agreement than in the marriage union. Why? Because no two people on earth can get any closer in their spirits than a man and a woman who are walking in unity with God in their marriage.

THERE'S NO GREATER POTENTIAL OF POWER OF AGREEMENT THAN IN THE MARRIAGE UNION.

Now, if you understand what great power there is in a married couple being in unity, you'll understand why the enemy fights marriage so hard. Marriage represents the greatest form of power possible when two people touch and agree and pray together. In this kind of agreement, Jesus said, "It will be done."

When we started out as a couple, the Lord told Sharon and me that we had to come into a place of agreement in our spirits, and we should never let anything break the power of that agreement. Of course, we have challenges because we are human. In fact, at times I think we're more human than anyone else! We've had to learn to forgive, to ask forgiveness, repent, show mercy, and receive mercy.

As Christian couples, we must determine to tear down the things in our marriages and families and in the Body of Christ that would keep us from coming into agreement. Then when you touch and agree for your children, you know the power of God is active.

Everyone needs someone to agree with them in prayer. If you're a single parent and you come into agreement with your children, you know the power of God is released.

Honoring Your Mate

Likewise, ye husbands, dwell with them according to knowledge, giving honour unto the wife, as unto the weaker vessel, and as being heirs together of the grace of life; that your prayers be not hindered.

1 Peter 3:7 KJV

To honor someone is to treat them the way you want to be treated. How do you want to be treated? Do you want to be treated like a king? Then treat your mate in the same manner. If you're the king, treat her like a queen. If you're the queen, treat him like a king. It is reciprocal and will come back to you.

Honoring and loving your spouse are two of the most important things you can do for your children. It's something they need to see you doing firsthand! Your children are constantly observing how you act and how you treat others. When they see your sincere, kind demonstrations of affection towards your spouse, they'll know they can expect to be treated well too. Love your spouse and watch your children respond.

HONORING AND LOVING YOUR SPOUSE ARE TWO OF THE MOST IMPORTANT THINGS YOU CAN DO FOR YOUR CHILDREN.

Never degrade or talk down to your spouse, especially in front of your children. Instead, build him or her up with praises on a consistent basis. Don't be fooled, our children hear every word and they notice how we treat one of their two most favorite people. It's equally important that our kids see us apologize to each other when one of us has been wrong. To do that takes a spirit of humility that allows us to admit our mistakes. Living with someone makes conflict inevitable sometimes. That's normal. But even during disagreements, we can choose to speak in a way that reflects our respect and love for that other person.

REMEMBER THAT TO SOME DEGREE OUR CHILDREN GET THEIR IMAGE OF GOD FROM THEIR EARTHLY PARENTS.

Yes, our children are watching and they're listening. Daughters form their image of how a man should treat them based on how their father treats their mother. Sons learn how they should treat women by the way they see their father treating their mother. Likewise, mothers are teaching their daughters how to love and honor their husbands. Remember, also, that to some degree our children get their image of God from their earthly parents.

101

Be of One Mind

Finally, be ye all of one mind....

1 Peter 3:8 KJV

It takes an effort to be of one mind (one in thought), but it's possible. Sharon and I dated for three years before we married (some of that time we were in different towns apart from each other), and we had an opportunity to develop our knowledge of one another through the mail and by phone.

We thought we knew each other, but we didn't know each other in the depth that we thought. Because we had made the decision to love each other, we were willing to get to know each other, even when it meant receiving correction from one another.

Over the years, we've grown in our communication, and we stay on the fifth level of communication where we talk intimately with each other. Many people don't have the ability to receive or give correction to each other. In order to give correction, you've got to be able to receive it. Always remember that principle, because too many times people are quick to give correction, but it's hard for them to receive it.

> IN ORDER TO GIVE CORRECTION, YOU'VE GOT TO BE ABLE TO RECEIVE IT.

The Bible says to get the log or beam out of your own eye, and then you'll be able to see clearly how to get the splinter out of the other person's eye. It won't seem as great to you when you're working on yourself to get rid of wrong attitudes and feelings. When you go to the other person, you'll go to them in meekness and humility if you have something to say to them.

Having Compassion One of Another

... having compassion one of another, love as brethren, be pitiful, be courteous.

1 Peter 3:8 KJV

To be *pitiful* means to "be sympathetic with each other." You need to be able to feel what your mate is going through. Then this verse says to be courteous with one another and I appreciate the fact that Sharon is courteous to me as I seek to do the same towards her.

Out of the abundance of the heart the mouth will speak. What's down inside your heart will come out in pressure situations. That's why it's important that you spend time with God on a daily basis. When you spend time with Him, then your time in relationships with other people will be strengthened by the Word. What's inside of you will come out in your attitude, words, and thoughts toward others.

Not Rendering Evil for Evil

Not rendering evil for evil, or railing for railing: but contrariwise blessing....

1 Peter 3:9 KJV

In other words, when someone does you wrong, just bless them and be good to them. Sow a blessing to them.

... knowing that ye are thereunto called, that ye should inherit a blessing.

1 Peter 3:9 KJV

If you'll sow a blessing to someone else, it will come back to you. Whatever you sow, you'll reap. (Galatians

103

6:7.) This is true in every area of life. Plant a seed of love when your mate is going through a difficult time, or when you're in a situation in which it looks like there's strife. Don't join in the strife with the other person. Sow mercy and love into that situation, and you'll see that person change right before your eyes. You will reap what you've sown. If you sow strife, then you'll get strife from the other person.

> ❧
>
> BEFORE WE REACT, IT'S IMPORTANT THAT WE STOP AND ASK OURSELVES, "HOW WOULD JESUS ACT IN THIS SITUATION?"
>
> ❧

Before we react, it's important that we stop and ask ourselves, "How would Jesus act in this situation?" Walk in the self-control of the Holy Spirit that you have inside of you. A lot of people say, "Well, I just don't have control. This is just my nature." No, it's not your nature! You have the Spirit of God to help you. When you were born again and engrafted into Christ, you received a new nature. But it's up to you to live out that new nature.

Before you take any action or speak any words, stop and get control of yourself. Then say, "Honey, I love you. Let's pray about this." Or say it in the way that fits your personality. Make sure that what comes from you are words of life, not words of destruction.

For he that will love life, and see good days, let him refrain his tongue from evil, and his lips that they speak no guile.

1 Peter 3:10 KJV

If you want to see good days in your marriage, refrain your tongue from speaking evil and deceit. If we will control our tongue from speaking in a detrimental way toward one another, many marriages can be saved. Stop and get control!

What to Do If You Are Divorced

Now, if you have already experienced the devastation of divorce know that God is a big God. He forgives divorce, heals broken hearts, and restores broken families. Being divorced is not God's best, but it does not mean that you have to give up to the enemy. You can still have a positive influence on your kids. What it means is that now you must be aware of the negative impact of the divorce and its effects on your children and then balance it off with God's grace, truth, and honesty.

If you are divorced, you need to ask God for His forgiveness and then forgive your former spouse and move on with your life. In spite of how your former spouse may be treating you, you need to show your children how to respond in love and grace (as Jesus does with us when we are difficult to love). When you have to deal with your former spouse, do it without rage or vengeance. Pray and ask God to give you the strength to stand strong for yourself and for your children. Romans 12:17-21 NIV admonishes us to:

Do not repay anyone evil for evil. Be careful to do what is right in the eyes of everybody. If it is possible, as far as it depends on you, live at peace with everyone. Do not take revenge, my friends, but leave room for God's wrath, for it is written: "It is mine to avenge; I will repay," says the Lord. On the contrary: "If your enemy is hungry, feed him; if he is thirsty, give him something to drink. In doing this, you will heap burning coals on his head." Do

not be overcome by evil, but overcome evil with good.

If you have gone through a divorce or are in a difficult marriage, you are in an excellent place to demonstrate to your children what it's like to turn your life around by giving it to God and letting Him be your Lord and then following His will for your life.

God hates divorce. His Word is clear and the fallout from divorce is almost always tragic. The statistics don't lie. Where there is divorce there is pain, depression, poverty, lower grades, higher crime, and higher "at risk" activities. Make no bones about it; divorce is not good, especially for our children. If your marriage is in trouble, do whatever it takes to get it healed!

Run from Evil

Let him eschew evil....

1 Peter 3:11 KJV

To eschew evil means to run from it. Run from evil situations. Run from the very appearance of evil. If you're in a situation that's a temptation to you, whether it's on your job or wherever it might be, listen to your heart and obey your spirit. Abstain from evil. Flee from the very appearance of evil that would try to pull you away from the good life found in Jesus Christ.

... and do good; let him seek peace, and ensue it.

1 Peter 3:11 KJV

Go after the good. Seek peace. It takes an effort in a marriage relationship to seek peace—to be a peacemaker, to be a peace maintainer—but you can do it, for the Peacemaker lives inside of you.

The Lord's Eyes and Ears Are Open to the Righteous

For the eyes of the Lord are over the righteous, and his ears are open unto their prayers: but the face of the Lord is against them that do evil.

1 Peter 3:12 KJV

When you are walking after God's will and making every effort to obey Him, God is open to hear you. But His face is against you if you're going after evil.

And who is he that will harm you, if ye be followers of that which is good?

1 Peter 3:13 KJV

This means that the enemy cannot have any place in your life. He can't harm you, he can't get through to your marriage, and he can't get into your life if you're following after that which is good. And having a strong, loving marriage will give security to your children. It will provide a solid example to them and help you to raise them to be champions for Him!

FAITH IN ACTION

Take some serious time to really reflect on the state of your marriage. See if there are any areas where work needs to be done. Remember, if changes need to be made, it must start with you. You initiate the change. First, ask God to help you to genuinely love and honor your spouse. As you pour yourself into them like Jesus poured Himself into us it will have an impact. Determine to protect your marriage at all costs. This is God's will! If you are a single parent, ask God to come in and be your spouse. He's more than able!

Possible Areas in My Marriage
that Need Improvement

- Praying for one another

  _____

- Speaking positive about each other

  _____

- Having fun and romancing each other

  _____

- Reconcile any differences

  _____

- Communication

  _____

- Am I serving with a Christ-like spirit?

  _____

"Do not let the sun go down while you are still angry" Ephesians 4:26 NIV.

"Whoever would love life and see good days must keep his tongue from evil and his lips from deceitful speech" 1 Peter 3:10 NIV.

"Husbands, in the same way be considerate as you live with your wives, and treat them with respect as the weaker partner and as heirs with you of the gracious gift of life, so that nothing will hinder your prayers" 1 Peter 3:7 NIV.

"She notices him, regards him, honors him, prefers him, venerates and esteems him; and that she defers to him, praises him, and loves and admires him exceedingly" Ephesians 5:33 AMP.

13 GUIDELINES FOR PARENTING

"For I have known him, in order that he may command his children and his household after him, that they keep the way of the LORD and do righteousness and justice...."

— *Genesis 18:19*

These are strong suggestions based on our many years of parenting and of pastoring. If followed, the relationships you have with your children will surely improve. Commit them to memory and start implementing them today; then watch them work for you and your children!

1. Set the Example

As parents, set the example so your children have something to follow. You can't set rules and regulations and then disobey them yourself.

2. Boundaries with Love

Jesus said that He didn't come to do away with the law, but He came to fulfill the law (Matthew 5:17), so don't do away with the boundaries, rules, and regulations, because they're necessary. But you must give love and build relationships with your children.

3. Share God's Word

We're to share the Word with our children as we go throughout the house, and we're to write the Word over the doorposts of our homes. Sit down and talk to your children about the Word.

"You shall love the Lord your God with all your heart, with all your soul, and with all your strength.

"And these words which I command you today shall be in your heart.

"You shall teach them diligently to your children, and shall talk of them when you sit in your house, when you walk by the way, when you lie down, and when you rise up.

"You shall bind them as a sign on your hand, and they shall be as frontlets between your eyes.

"You shall write them on the doorposts of your house and on your gates."

Deuteronomy 6:5-9

4. Listen

Most parents need to work on this one! James 1:19 says, *"Let every man be swift to hear, slow to speak, slow to wrath."* It takes effort to listen to children and teenagers, to get down on their level, to be able to relate to them and really listen to what they're saying, but it's very important to them.

5. Quality Time

God dealt with me when Sarah was a baby that time with my children was not lost time. It was invested time, and it was quality time. I used to think that what was important was the time I spent in ministry, but then God began to reorient my priorities to include time with my family. I had to reorient myself to learn to play with Strawberry Shortcake and Lemon Meringue dolls and make pies and eat whatever Sarah and Ruthie cooked!

Sometimes parents think they're spending time with the children when they go home and turn on the TV set. That's not quality time. Quality time is when you pay individual attention to your children, sharing with them, and listening to them.

If you'll build a relationship with your children when they are small, when they get older, they'll want to have time with you. When the girls were small and I was playing barrettes with my girls, letting them literally cover my head with barrettes, my first thought was, *Surely, I've got better things to do.* Then the Lord let me know, "This is where you need to be and this is one of the most important ministries you will ever do."

The "macho image," which the world has projected upon men, implies that if you're going to be a man, you need to distance yourself from little children and refrain from crying and being tender. God hasn't called us to be like the god of this world. He has called us to be like Jesus who said, *"Let the little children come to Me, and do not forbid them; for of such is the kingdom of heaven"* (Matthew 19:14). Then, *"He laid His hands on them . . ."* (v. 15).

When the kids were growing up, I'd help put them to bed at night. On one particular occasion when I put the boys to bed, John was out like a light, but Paul just lay there. He said, "Daddy."

"Yes, Paul."

"I love you."

"I love you, too, Paul."

Then he said, "Why don't you come in here and love me then?"

I had already hugged him, kissed him, prayed with him, and read the Bible. There was a need in his life to be touched. Every child needs to be touched and ministered to with the love of God. As a parent, you have the power to minister love. Of course, I hugged him again and told him how I loved him.

My greatest joy, outside of the Lord and worshipping Him, is my family. I love to be with my family. I love my wife. We're a team. I love my children. If you're going to be a parent who raises champions for God, then you've got to learn to spend time with your children and do what they like to do.

How do we save children from getting on drugs and alcohol? If the deepest needs of their life are met, especially when they're small, they won't look for destructive ways to get those needs met. They won't be vulnerable to those things. When basic needs are not met, children often search in every avenue they can. In a study that took place on the West Coast with prostitutes, it was discovered that over 95 percent of them came from families where there was no positive father image. What were they seeking in prostitution? A craving for what they never received at home.

Where there has been a void, there's a greater tendency to become involved in homosexuality. For the greatest percentage of the young boys involved in homosexuality, either there was an absentee father or a father who lacked spiritual fortitude. "The sins of the fathers," the Scripture says, "will be visited to the third and fourth generation." When there's a breakdown in the family, it doesn't just affect the fathers. It can affect four generations of families. Are you beginning to see the importance of letting the Lord build our marriages and homes? If you are a single mom, ask Jesus to come in and be a father to your children. He will come in and make a way where there seems to be no way. He can and will do miracles!

6. Be Quick to Ask Forgiveness

James 5:16 says, *"Confess your trespasses to one another, and pray for one another, that you may be healed."* Be quick to humble yourself and ask forgiveness of your children when you've made a mistake. When your children see you humbling yourself before God and asking for forgiveness, it sets a pattern for them to follow.

7. Laughter

A good laugh will set you free from pent-up emotions. After we disciplined our children, we would love them and say, "You'd better put on a happy face." The children couldn't help but smile, and then we would laugh. Sometimes we'd laugh about things and they didn't even know what we were laughing about, but we'd all get tickled. Laughter is like medicine.

Because we've tried to fill our home with laughter, there have been some pretty hilarious moments down through the years. Once, when the boys were about four or five, we were teaching them about how we came up with their names. Our children's names come directly from the Bible. They each have an Old Testament name and a New Testament name. The boys, John Samuel and Paul David, go from the New Testament to the Old. The girls, Ruth Anna and Sarah Elizabeth, go from the Old Testament to the New.

So, we were explaining to the boys how God had given us their first and second names. John and Paul represented apostles from the New Testament. Then, we told them how the prophet Samuel in the Old Testament had anointed David with oil. Well, they got it, because one day when Sharon and I walked in the kitchen, Paul was kneeling down and John was holding a half empty bottle of Wesson oil that he'd just dumped on Paul's head. "What's going on?" we asked. John answered, "Well, I'm the prophet and he's the apostle and I'm anointing him." Except he called Paul the "opossum" instead of the "apostle." So, he was anointed and we all had a good laugh.

8. Fairness

Children are all different, and as parents, we should never compare them. Each child will have separate gifts and personality traits which you as a parent should encourage and develop. Each child will require different handling. However, when it comes to the boundaries, rules, and love, all children should be treated equally according to their ages.

9. Correction in Love

The *most* loving thing you will ever do for your children is to discipline them. Like God does with us, our reason for disciplining our children is because we love them and desire to see godly character developed in them. The goal in discipline and correction should always be character development: training our children in the principles of godly character. The process of correction will produce godly fruit.

> ≈
>
> THE GOAL IN DISCIPLINE AND CORRECTION SHOULD ALWAYS BE CHARACTER DEVELOPMENT.
>
> ≈

10. Trust God—Let Go

Sometimes parents tend to overprotect their children. Sometimes parents feel like they've got to be every place the children are, which is a spirit of fear. There's a point where you have to let go and trust God, believing that the training you've instilled in them will preserve and keep them.

It's so important to pray and intercede for your children. We've had many examples where parents have either seen into the spirit or were quickened by the Spirit to pray for their children. Because of prayer, the enemy was stopped from destroying or coming against their lives.

11. Build God-Confidence, Not Self-Confidence

As a parent raising champion children, we need to instill in them not self-confidence, but a biblically based God-confidence. It's a God-confidence that acknowledges special God-given gifts, talents, and abilities. It's a God-confidence that God will help them to develop and use those abilities if they are submitted to Him. It's a God-confidence that will supernaturally rise up in our kids in special times of need.

A great example is how God used Sarah on a mission trip in Ecuador. They had a youth service one night and the arena was jam-packed with kids everywhere. Hundreds of them got saved and the pastor gave the altar call and then he called Sarah up to pray for people to be healed and delivered. Sarah was holding the electric microphone and when she picked up the chain, the electrical current inside the microphone went right through her body and she began to shake uncontrollably. Her eyes rolled back, and she said that when the electrical shock went through her, she could feel the fillings in her teeth and her ring ripped through the skin on her finger. Sarah thought she was gone. But a God-confidence rose up in her and she began to scream out, "Jesus! Jesus!" and the second time she said His name, she was able to let go of that chain. They took Sarah off stage and when she came to, she said, "I realized what had happened and I knew that the devil had tried to kill me in what I was destined for."

Bill Gothard made the statement, "I will live and not die until my work on earth is finished."

Sarah said, "I knew I hadn't fulfilled my God-given destiny so I went back on the stage and I just said to the crowd, "The thief comes to steal, to kill you, and to destroy you. Jesus comes to give you life. Moments ago I was nearly electrocuted through an electrical short in the microphone, but Jesus gave me life. Tonight, I am giving you an invitation to receive eternal life."

She called one of Victory's teenagers up, Jonathan Coussens, who had almost lost his leg in the past year-

and-a-half because of a cancerous growth. Doctors thought they were going to have to amputate his leg. His mother is a R.N. and she and his father are members of our church. They prayed and stood on the Word and saw God heal his knee and leg so no amputation was required. Sarah had Jonathan give his testimony.

Then Sarah gave an invitation for those who wanted to be delivered from drugs, alcohol, sexual immorality, and every kind of bondage that had been on their lives. One man counted 1,500 (before he lost count) of those who walked forward at the invitation. God moved in a mighty way and empowered Sarah and Jonathan with His God-confidence.

"I can do all things through Christ who strengthens me."

Philippians 4:13

"Being confident of this, that he who began a good work in you will carry it on to completion until the day of Christ Jesus."

Philippians 1:6 NIV

12. Strike When the Iron Is Hot

This principle focuses on timing. While there is probably no "wrong" time for sharing spiritual truth with our children, some moments are more conducive to learning than others, and it is a wise parent who knows the difference. They will seize those special moments realizing that they afford an opportunity to shape their child's worldview.

The old-timers used to call that "striking when the iron is hot." The phrase itself came out of the village blacksmith's shop and referred to that moment when the iron was white hot and capable of being shaped by the blacksmith. It only lasted a moment, and once the iron cooled off it had to be reheated before the blacksmith could finish his work. So it is with a child and spiritual instruction.

In addition to those special moments, spiritual training for our children should also include a regular devotional time. This scheduled instruction—family worship, if you please—sets the spiritual tone. While it may not have as dramatic an impact as one of those "strike when the iron is hot" experiences, its importance cannot be overemphasized. It prepares the child's heart, lays a firm foundation, and establishes a holy habit of spiritual discipline. In truth, the spiritual formation of our children requires both regular instruction and spontaneous moments.

Some of the most important spiritual training your child will ever receive will probably happen spontaneously as you spend time together. That being the case, determine right now, before God, that you will make time with your children your highest priority.[9]

"These commandments that I give you today are to be upon your hearts. Impress them on your children. Talk about them when you sit at home and when you walk along the road, when you lie down and when you get up. Tie them as symbols on your hands and bind them on your foreheads. Write them on the doorframes of your houses and on your gates."

Deuteronomy 6:6-9 NIV

[9]Richard Exley, *The Making of a Man* (Tulsa, OK: Honor Books, 1993), 75.

13. Make Home a Refuge

As parents raising champions for God, we need to make home a haven—a refuge where our kids like to hang out. A place they'll miss when they're gone, not someplace they'll remember with grief. We must work to make our homes places where our kids can retreat when they need comfort and acceptance, regardless of their age. They should feel safe at home no matter what's going on in the outside world. They need to be able to relax and let down their guard.

We should strive to make our homes centers of compassion and hope for our children, not sources of pain and frustration. The physical structure of a home doesn't have to be fancy or crammed with all the latest technology. It simply needs to be warm, restful, filled with love, and the Spirit of God.

We need to remember that God formed the HOME before government, school, or the church. It is not the place of the government to raise your children. It's not the school's place to train them in the way they should go, nor does this responsibility fall on the church. All three of these institutions have tried to pick up the shattered fragments of boys and girls who have been ripped apart because of the neglect of their parents to build a place called home.

If your deepest desire is to raise your children God's way, to raise champions for Him, then you must see the importance of the home environment. While you do not have the power from within yourself to build all godly homes in the world, you do have the power to build one at your address. Go for it! Dedicate yourself to preparing a place for your child that will impact his life for all eternity.

FAITH IN ACTION

Reflect on these above points and write down specific areas where you need improvement. Then, ask God to strengthen you in those areas. Again, write down the thoughts that the Holy Spirit brings to your mind. Pray the following: Lord, I confess to You that my children are blessed because of You. They will be like trees planted by streams of water. They will bear fruit at the right time, and everything they do will prosper! Thank You, God, that my children will know You and will do great exploits for Your Kingdom. They will be strong and of good courage. You are with them wherever they go. Your Spirit is being poured out upon my children every day and You are empowering me to be the parent that You called me to be!

Areas I Need Improvement

1)_____

2)_____

3)_____

4)_____

"He has blessed your children within you" Psalm 147:13.

"There is hope in your future, says the Lord, that your children shall come back to their own border" Jeremiah 31:17.

"Blessed is the man who walks not in the counsel of the ungodly, nor stands in the path of sinners, nor sits in the seat of the scornful; but his delight is in the law of the Lord, and in His law he meditates day and night. He shall be like a tree planted by the rivers of water, that brings forth its fruit in its season, whose leaf also shall not wither; and whatever he does shall prosper" Psalm 1:1-3.

"Here am I and the children whom the Lord has given me! We are for signs and wonders in Israel from the Lord of hosts . . ." Isaiah 8:18.

a. Sarah's first Christmas.

b. Reading Bible stories to Sarah & Ruthie at Christmas.

c. Putting together the girls' Christmas present before Christmas morning.

d. Family Christmas card – December 1985.

a. Sarah (not shown) & Ruthie fixing their dad's hair.

b. Sarah, Ruthie, John, & Paul playing in living room.

c. October 27, 1991 – The Sunday after the house fire at the morning service in the Mabee Center. Taking a moment to thank God for His protection and deliverance.

d. John (standing) & Paul (sitting) in the backyard, though Paul was not having as much fun as John.

a. Sarah ministering on mission trip in High School.

b. Ruthie ministering on mission trip in High School.

c. Family Christmas card – December 1998.

d. John & Paul doing yard work with Dad at Gran Gran's house.

a. Sarah ministering in Hong Kong.

b. Ruthie leading worship at a Victory service.

c. John ministering at 24-7 youth event.

d. Paul singing with his band enVoy at a youth rally.

a. Paul, Sarah, John, & Caleb – playing skeetball – Summer vacation 2004.

b. Daugherty Kids – December 2006.

c. John, Ruthie, & Paul enjoying some ice cream and laughs – Winter 2003.

d. Sharon's dad Clyde, mother Ella Vee, & Billy Joe's mother Iru.

a. Family with Gran Gran –
May 2008.

b. Five generations together
– Sharon's grandmother,
Sharon's mom holding
Elizabeth, Sharon, & Sarah –
December 2007.

c. Paul, Sharon, Billy Joe,
John, & Adam with "Bugs
Life" glasses on during
Vacation in Disney World –
May 2005.

a. Adam & Ruthie at Dallas Cowboys game – September 2008.

b. Fishing on Skiatook Lake – June 2007.

c. Family Vacation in Florida – June 2007.

a. Family Christmas card – December 2008.

b. With grandchildren Isaac 3$^1/_2$ years & Elizabeth 16 months – January 2009.

c. Caleb, Sarah, Isaac, & Elizabeth in Hong Kong – November 2008.

11

A FINAL THOUGHT, A FINAL PROMISE

"His descendants will be mighty on earth...."
— *Psalm 112:2*

This is one of the promises that I speak to kids when I see them: *You mighty man*, or *How are you doing, you mighty woman of faith?* Many children don't even understand what I am really saying, but that's okay. One day they will. God didn't give you children to raise up as losers. He gave you children to raise up as champions for Him. This book has helped you to get the vision and has equipped you with the tools so you can begin to see that reality take place. Now begin to declare it before them and God.

> ঌ
>
> No matter how old your children are, it's never too late to believe God that they are going to be mighty upon the earth.
>
> ঌ

Maybe your children are already grown. So what. It's never too late

123

to believe God that they are going to be mighty upon the earth. You may look at your own life and say, *"I haven't been too mighty in the days gone by, but Lord, I'm one of Your children, so I am going to be mighty upon the earth."* It should be revelation to us that God has a great plan for each of His children.

Psalm 115:14 says, *"May the Lord give you increase more and more, you and your children."* God's plan for Abraham was that he would expand. His plan for Isaac was that he would go beyond Abraham. His plan for Jacob, who became Israel, was that he would go beyond both Abraham and Isaac. His plan for the twelve sons of Israel was that they would go beyond Abraham, Isaac, and Israel. It is God's will that you, as His child, multiply and increase.

God Has Blessed Your Children

Psalm 147:13 says, *"He has blessed your children within you."* This is speaking about Jerusalem, Zion, and the people of God and that is who we are. He has blessed us and our children.

> THE SPIRIT OF GOD IS BEING POURED OUT UPON MY CHILDREN EVERY DAY.

Acts 2:17 says, *"And it shall come to pass in the last days, says God, that I will pour out of My Spirit on all flesh; your sons and your daughters shall prophesy...."* Declare over your children: *The Spirit of God is being poured out upon my children every day.*

In my prayer life, I thank God for His promises: *Lord, I thank You that Your Spirit is being poured out upon Caleb and Sarah, Isaac and Lizzie, Adam and*

Ruthie, John and Paul, and upon all the children in Victory and in Victory Christian School, and all the outreach ministries as well as around the world. In the Spirit, these children are our children. We are believing God for them.

Declare that Your Children Are Champions

What happens when you speak the Word of God and stand upon it? That Word becomes alive and active in the earth in relationship to your faith. It will be unto you according to your faith. God has made that very clear. He puts no limits on faith, and faith should put no limits on God. Turn your faith loose for your children. Declare them to be champions for Him!

Acts 16:31 is a powerful promise to every believer and is the scripture I want to leave you with. *"Believe on the Lord Jesus Christ, and you will be saved, you and your household."* It is God's promise to you that every one of your children and grandchildren be saved, filled with the Holy Spirit, blessed, increased, prospered, never begging for bread, and mighty upon the earth.

The family is critically important in the plan of God, and raising champions for Him is a holy and honorable calling that we must take seriously. Now, go do it and be blessed!

Staying the Course
8 Quick Reminders
for Disciplining Champions

Be encouraged! You are not alone! God is giving you strength to be a godly parent. Just as you desire to raise godly children for Him, He wants to help you to do it. I encourage you to read through these eight steps on a regular basis. Although they are by no means a complete list, they cover a few of the major areas of concern in the discipline of children.

1. Be consistent. This is probably the biggest challenge a parent faces. Nevertheless, it's a major key in effective discipline. If children know there is going to be consistency in the discipline, then they will stop at the boundary line set by the parents. Children need boundaries for security. Children with no boundaries are basically left to themselves and run out of control. There is no security in their lives.

Boundary lines for children are like fences or places of protection. I remember hearing the story of a school playground which had no fence around it. The playground was located next to a busy street with cars continually whizzing by. The children stayed close to the school building while this huge playground remained empty. School officials couldn't get the children to use it all. Finally, a fence was put up at the edge of the property. Once the fence was up, the children played on the entire playground because there was a boundary which made them feel secure and protected.

> IF CHILDREN KNOW THERE IS GOING TO BE CONSISTENCY IN THE DISCIPLINE, THEN THEY WILL STOP AT THE BOUNDARY LINE SET BY THE PARENTS.

It's the same with children in the family. When there are boundaries of correction they are free to expand and release themselves in development and in educational and spiritual experiences that are positive.

2. Discipline immediately. You have perhaps viewed a child being beaten by an angry and frustrated

126

parent who's yelling, "I've told you a thousand times not to do that!" Well, the time to correct them is after the first time, not the thousandth.

Establish the rules or boundaries. If the rules are broken, then with no anger or animosity, go to the child and say, "What was the rule? What did I tell you to do or not to do?" Explain to them what was violated and immediately correct them.

When a parent disciplines immediately, instead of anger being instilled in the child, a bond of love will be formed in the parent-child relationship. Hug the child after you discipline them, reassuring them of your love.

If a child gets away with breaking the rules, rebellion will build in their heart and a barrier will come between the child and parent. If that rebellion is not removed, the child will carry it inside and be alienated from the parents. But if there's immediate discipline when a child is small, the spirit of rebellion will have no place in them.

3. Discipline for instant obedience. A child can be trained to obey after the third time he is told, or he can be trained to obey after the first time. It all depends on the trainer. Your children will be disciplined upon the basis of your level of tolerance or intolerance. They will rise to a standard or they will fall to it, depending where you set it. If children don't learn to obey parents, they will have tremendous difficulty obeying the Word of God.

4. Don't allow your child to cause a breakdown of authority between you and your mate. There's a breakdown in authority where either a husband or a wife will not back the authority of the other. If Sharon says something, even if I don't agree with it, or if I say something and she doesn't agree with me, we back the authority of the other. If you don't, you'll have rebellion. First Samuel 15:23 says, *"Rebellion is as the sin of witchcraft. . . ."*

If the husband and wife don't support each other, they open the door for the enemy to attack their children. Suddenly, there are all types of manifestations of evil and the parents wonder, "Where did this come in? We take our children to church every Sunday. We've done this, and we've done that." There must be unity and harmony between the husband and wife to support one another's authority.

5. The husband, as head of the home, should take the lead role of disciplinarian. God set Jesus as Head of the Church, and He set the husband as head of the home. God ordained the man to be the head of the family. The husband is to take the lead and the load.

But what has happened? Because many husbands have abdicated their place of leadership, women have had to rise up and become strong. God intended for both the husband and the wife to be strong. An acclaimed speaker and author, the late Dr. Edwin Louis Cole said, "God created the husband and wife, not to compete, but to complete each other."

In our case, Sharon and I both disciplined the children, although I usually took the leadership role. There are times when it's not comfortable to discipline, but it's always expedient. Many men don't want to be the disciplinarian, either because they aren't strong enough spiritually or because they lose control of their anger too easily.

God hasn't given men a spirit of timidity. If discipline has to take place in the home, then do it. Rise up to your calling. Discipline always brings the peaceable fruit of righteousness. What happens when you don't have discipline in the home? You have the unpeaceable fruit of unrighteousness and the manifestation of wickedness. In situations where there's no father in the home, the mother must assume the role of disciplinarian. Mom, you can do it!

6. Show respect. If we disrespect our kids, they will in turn disrespect us and others. A common way we as parents disrespect our children is by letting them get away with being disrespectful to us. If we take it lightly when they are disrespectful to us or refuse to correct them, we are actually showing disrespect to them. Children need guidance, but unless our guidance stems from love and respect, it will come off as nothing but orders. As a parent we owe it to our kids to guide them into being respectful children. Otherwise they will grow to be disrespectful to all authority.

7. Show genuine love. Jesus said in John 15:12 NIV, *"My command is this: Love each other as I have loved you."* This command applies equally to our children. How did Jesus love us? He gave Himself up for us and He did so because of genuine love. There will be times when we will have to give ourselves up for our children. That may come in the form of time, attention, and understanding. Children can't grow into healthy, well-adjusted adults unless they have been genuinely loved by their parents. They must know that they are unique and important or they won't be able to get past the need for affirmation in their lives. If they don't get it at home, they will seek to find it in drugs, bad relationships, and rebellion. They won't be properly equipped emotionally or spiritually to stand up to peer pressure and the temptations of the world.

8. Know Your Parenting Rights. You have rights as a parent. However, only you can stand up for yourself and these rights. When you do, you take a giant step towards being a better leader for your children.

You have the right to:

- **Take care of yourself**, for this will help you take better care of your child and others. Eat right, get adequate rest, exercise, take time out, and remember sometimes it's okay to say "no" to family and friends, when you are overloaded with demands.

- **Seek help from others.** Call your pastor, doctor, or other professionals if you have a concern that is creating havoc in your family.

- **Get control and express your feelings in an appropriate manner.** Don't forget that you are the family's manager. Set the home rules, and expect your children to follow them.

- **Reject attempts by your child to manipulate you through anger or peer pressure.** Be a "united front" with your spouse as you hold strong to rules.

- **Receive respect, forgiveness, affection, and acceptance.** These attributes are expected in functional families, and you have the duty to teach your child how to treat you justly.

- **Offer respect, forgiveness, affection, and acceptance.** The best way for a child to learn these attributes is for you to role model them.

- **Maintain a full personal life so that when your child grows up and leaves home, you will not be lost.** Cultivate your marriage and other interests so that your latter days will be fulfilling.

- **Stay involved in church and attend regularly.** Make spiritual nourishment important to your family so that you have a source of strength when facing life's interruptions.[10]

---

[10]Robert & Debra Bruce and Ellen W. Oldacre, *Guilt-free Parenting* (Nashville: Dimensions, 1997), 102.

FAITH IN ACTION

Prayer is faith in action. The following is a prayer for your children. You can pray it every day, sometimes many times a day! After prayer, speak God's promises over your children.

Pray: *Father, I thank You that the outpouring of the Holy Spirit is upon each of our children. Our sons and daughters are delivered. The seed of the righteous are blessed, prospered, enriched, fulfilled, satisfied, and increased.*

Lord, we thank You that our children will prophesy according to Acts 2:17. The Word will not depart out of the mouth of our seed or out of the mouth of our seed's seed. Our children are for signs and wonders. We decree it. All of our children will be taught of the Lord and great will be their peace.

Lord, we raise the hedge of protection around them, that shield of faith. No weapon formed against our family, our home, our lives will prosper. And Lord, even where children have been taken into the hand of the enemy, You said You would deliver them from the prey of the terrible. You said You would bring them from the north, south, east, and west. Sons and daughters will come and nurse at Your side, so we call them back home. Prodigal sons, prodigal daughters, prodigal grandchildren, come home. We loose you from the hand of the enemy. We say our children are blessed. Everything our hands touch is blessed and we touch our children by faith.

No darkness will overtake our children. No deception will lay hold of them. No part of the curse can latch onto them. No sin, no sickness, no poverty, no disease, no death can take them. We decree it by the blood of the Lord Jesus Christ, they are delivered and set free to make a difference for God's Kingdom in the earth. Amen!

SCRIPTURAL CONFESSIONS
FOR YOUR CHAMPIONS

The Bible is filled with promises from God which we can pray and speak over our children. If you are speaking God's Word over them, you know you are speaking in line with His will. Speak the following confessions daily over your children. Let the Word become alive in your heart. Let it become the true reality as you stand in faith for His promises to be fulfilled in every area of their lives. His Word never fails!

Insert the name(s) of the child(ren) for whom you are making the following confessions in the blanks provided. Make the confessions aloud.

Before you begin, please pray with me: *Father, I know You have said in Your Word that faith works by love* (Galatians 5:6). *We love You, Lord. Because of Your love in us as parents* (or guardians), *we love our children. Thank You for Your mercy being poured out on our family and on our home. Thank You for a fresh anointing on us to stand in the gap for our children. We place a prayer covering over our entire family, Lord. Thank You for the rain of righteousness pouring on our family. Thank You also that Your angels keep guard over us and our children. In Jesus' name we pray. Amen.*

ACCEPTED . . .

_____is highly valued and accepted by God. To be accepted in Christ means that He esteems you very highly. _____ is valued and loved and has no fear of rejection!

Ephesians 1:6

APPROVAL . . .

_____is approved of the Lord. He/she is confident and secure in the love of the Lord and his/her parents with no need to seek the approval of man. Before God formed _____ in the womb, He knew him/her and He approved of him/her as one of His chosen instruments. Because of His approval of _____, He has entrusted him/her with the gospel!

2 Corinthians 10:18
Jeremiah 1:5 AMP
1 Thessalonians 2:4 AMP

ASSOCIATIONS . . .

_____ uses wisdom in selecting friends and with whom he/she spends his/her time. He/she chooses godly friends knowing that godly associations encourage the development of good habits. _____ is known by his/her actions because his/her conduct is pure and right.

1 Corinthians 15:33
Proverbs 20:11
Proverbs 27:17

BLESSED . . .

The Lord has commanded His blessing upon
_____. He/she is blessed coming in and going out.
That means at school, his/her job, his/her finances,
his/her health, and in every area of life His blessing is
coming upon him/her and overtaking him/her. Wherever he/she goes and whatever he/she does _____
will be blessed. His blessing makes _____ rich
and He adds no sorrow to it.

Deuteronomy 28:8,12
Proverbs 10:22

_____ walks in the counsel of the godly and in
the path of the righteous. His/her delight is in the law
of the Lord and in His law he/she meditates day and
night establishing a godly foundation for his/her life.
_____is obedient to the Lord and His Word and
so bears fruit in each season of his/her life.

Psalm 1:1-2

The Lord is _____'s shepherd. Because of that
he/she lacks no good thing. God gives him/her peaceful
rest, and He restores his/her soul. He leads him/her in
the path of righteousness. Even though _____
walks through the shadow of death he/she will fear no
evil, for God is with him/her. He/She is comforted by
His Word and His Spirit. God even prepares a table
before him/her in the presence of his/her enemies.
His/Her cup runs over with blessing and abundance.
Goodness and mercy follow _____ each day.
He/She will dwell in the house of the Lord forever.

Psalm 23

CARES/WORRIES/ANXIETIES/CONCERNS . . .

_____ is free from worry, anxiety, and concern. He/She learns to cast his/her concerns and challenges upon the Lord for He cares for _____ affectionately and watchfully. Every burden which tries to weigh _____ down, he/she gives to the Lord in prayer and God will sustain him/her. The Lord will never allow _____ to be moved—made to slip, fall, or fail.

1 Peter 5:7 AMP
Psalm 55:22 AMP

COMMON SENSE AND WISDOM . . .

_____ is full of the wisdom of the Lord. God has given to him/her a treasure of common sense because he/she is honest. He is a shield to him/her because he/she walks with integrity. So _____ understands what is right, just, and fair. He/she will not stumble along the path of life for the Holy Spirit is guiding him/her and he/she will find the right way to go.

Proverbs 2:7-9

_____ makes wise choices that keep him/her safe from harm. He/She embraces God's Word and His understanding and it keeps him/her safe in every situation. As _____ hides the Word of God in his/her heart, wisdom is entering his/her heart and mind and knowledge will fill him/her with joy.

Proverbs 2:10-12

COURAGEOUS . . .

_____ is strong and courageous. God will never leave him/her or forsake him/her. The Word of God does not depart from _____'s mouth. He/She meditates in it day and night gaining wisdom, strength, courage, and boldness. Because _____ knows who he/she is in Christ he/she is as bold as a lion and will do mighty things for Him.

Joshua 1:5-9 NIV
Proverbs 28:1

DELIVERANCE . . .

The Lord is delivering _____ from __(fill in the blank)_____ (situations, wrong relationships, unhealthy habits, etc.). When he/she calls upon the Lord, He will answer him/her. The Lord will be with _____ in trouble and will deliver him/her and honor him/her. The Lord will satisfy _____ and show him/her His salvation.

Psalm 91:14-16

DESTINY . . .

God has a special destiny for _____'s life. His plans are to prosper him/her and not to harm him/her, to give him/her hope and a future. The Lord is guiding _____ along the best pathway for his/her life. He will advise him/her and watch over him/her so that he/she fulfills his/her God-given destiny.

Jeremiah 29:11 NIV
Psalm 32:8
John 16:13

DILIGENT . . .

_____ is a hard worker and diligent. This diligence brings both spiritual and physical riches as God blesses the work of his/her hands. The Word says that "diligence" is a precious possession. It will lead to peace.

Proverbs 10:4
Psalm 90:17
Proverbs 13:4
Proverbs 21:5
2 Peter 3:14

DIRECTION . . .

_____ may plan his/her way in his/her own mind, but the Lord is directing his/her steps. Even when he/she stumbles, he/she will not fall, for the Lord will hold him/her up. _____ is always at the right place at the right time because he/she is led by the Lord.

Proverbs 16:9
Proverbs 20:24
Proverbs 24:16

DISCIPLINE . . .

_____ learns from correction and is wise. His/Her heart is open to hear constructive criticism from us and from the Lord and so he/she will be at home among the wise. _____ honors us as parents. He/she is obedient and pleasing to the Lord, and God will satisfy him/her with a long, peaceful, and happy life!

Proverbs 15:5

Proverbs 15:31
Hebrews 12:5 NIV
Colossians 3:20
Ephesians 6:2-3
Proverbs 23:13-14

EDUCATION . . .

_____ is a diligent student. God has given to him/her knowledge and skill in all learning and an unusual aptitude for understanding. _____ has great peace and is taught of the Lord. Thank You, Father, that You are blessing the works of his/her hands. He/She has the mind of Christ and finds favor and good understanding in the sight of God and man.

Daniel 1:9,17
Isaiah 54:13
Psalm 90:17
1 Corinthians 2:16
Proverbs 3:4

ENCOURAGEMENT . . .

_____ can do all things through Christ who strengthens him/her. Discouragement is far from him/her. Instead he/she learns to encourage himself/herself in the Lord and he/she will have great peace.

Philippians 4:13

God is with _____ and He is for him/her. He is his/her God and He will strengthen him/her, help him/her, and uphold him/her with His righteous right hand. He will perfect everything that concerns _____.

Romans 8:31
Isaiah 41:10-13
Psalm 138:8

EXCELLENT SPIRIT . . .

    Like Daniel, _____ has an excellent spirit!
Greater is He that is in _____ than he that is in
the world. Because he/she has an excellent spirit,
_____ will do great exploits for the Kingdom of
God.

Daniel 5:12
1 John 4:4
Daniel 11:32

FAITH . . .

    _____ walks by faith and not by sight. He/She
is not moved by what he/she sees in the world around
him/her, but instead allows the spirit of faith—believing and speaking God's Word—to dominate his/her
thoughts and words. Because he/she trusts in You,
he/she can say to the mountains that stand in his/her
way to be cast in the sea and they must move.
_____'s faith works effectively because he/she is
living and walking in the God-kind of love.

2 Corinthians 4:13,18
Galatians 5:6
Mark 10:23-24
2 Corinthians 5:7

FAMILY . . .

    Our family gets along well and we enjoy spending
time together. Our home is a place of peace and joy.

Our children are open in their communication with us, their parents. They are faithful, always responsible, and completely trustworthy. They have a good relationship with their siblings and will maintain those friendships throughout their lives. In our family we have made the decision to serve the Lord, a decision that will be passed down from generation to generation.

Isaiah 32:18
Daniel 6:4
Joshua 24:15

FAVOR . . .

God has blessed _____ and surrounded him/her with favor like a shield. Like Jesus, _____ is increasing in full understanding, in stature and years and favor with God and man.

Psalm 5:12
Proverbs 12:2
Luke 2:52

FEAR . . .

The faith of God and His Word in _____ conquers any fear that would try to come against him/her. God has given him/her a spirit of power and of love and of a sound mind. _____ walks free from fear because he/she trusts in the Lord. He/She sets his/her heart on Him and he/she will not be troubled.

Isaiah 54:14
2 Timothy 1:7
Psalm 34:17

God is for _____ so who can be against him/her? He/She has no reason to be afraid, for God will oppose those who oppose him/her and fight those who fight against him/her. _____ is able to sleep peacefully for the Lord will keep him/her safe.

Romans 8:31
Exodus 14:13-14
Psalm 35:1
Psalm 3:5
Psalm 4:8

FORGIVENESS ...

_____ chooses to walk in forgiveness. He/She does not hold on to offenses and takes no notice when others have treated him/her wrong. Because he/she chooses to forgive he/she receives the forgiveness of the Lord and his/her heart remains at peace.

1 Corinthians 13:5
John 20:23

FRUIT BEARING ...

In Christ, _____ has strength, abundance, and energy for every task. It is in Him that _____ lives and moves and has his/her being. _____ abides in Jesus and He abides in him/her and so he/she is productive in all he/she does for the Kingdom!

Acts 17:28
John 15:1-7

FRUIT OF THE SPIRIT ...

_____ is overflowing with the fruit of the Spirit—love, joy, peace, longsuffering, kindness, goodness, faithfulness, gentleness, and self-control. These attributes are increasing in his/her life each day replacing the works of the old nature. _____ walks by the Spirit and leaves no room for the works of the flesh in his/her life! Hallelujah!

Galatians 5:16-23

GIFTING . . .

The gift that God has placed within _____ makes room for him/her and brings him/her before great men. This gifting will bring great honor to the Lord as well.

Proverbs 18:16

GOD'S WORD . . .

_____ delights in reading and meditating on the Word of God. The Word of God is a firm foundation for his/her life providing a rich store of salvation, wisdom, and knowledge. Your Word, O Lord, guides him/her and enables him/her to be successful in all he/she does. Because _____ trusts in Your Word, he/she will not be afraid or discouraged for You are with him/her wherever he/she goes.

Joshua 1:7-9
Isaiah 33:6

Your Word is a lamp to _____'s feet and a light to his/her path. _____ hides Your Word in his/her heart so that he/she will choose right paths and turn from that which is not of You.

Psalm 119:11,105

GUIDANCE . . .

The Holy Spirit, the Spirit of truth, is guiding _____ into all truth and will show him/her things to come. As _____ seeks Your will for his/her life, You said You would reveal to him/her remarkable secrets about his/her future and Your plan for his/her life. He/She will listen to Your advice as You watch over him/her.

John 16:13
Jeremiah 33:3
Psalm 32:8

The Lord is directing _____'s path because he/she trusts in Him and does not lean to his/her own understanding. He/She acknowledges the Lord in all he/she does and so He will make his/her paths straight and secure.

Proverbs 3:5-6

God's Word keeps _____ when he/she sleeps, talks to him/her when he/she wakes up, and guides him/her in the way he/she should go.

Proverbs 6:20-23

HEALING AND WHOLENESS . . .

_____ is not wise in his/her own eyes, but instead he/she fears the Lord and turns away from evil. This will bring healing for his/her body and strength for his/her bones.

Proverbs 3:7-8

The law of the Spirit of life in Christ Jesus has set _____ free from the law of sin and death. In Christ, he/she is healed and whole.

Proverbs 3:7-8
Romans 8:2

_____ is healthy mentally, physically, and emotionally. Thank You that You shield him/her from harmful words, actions, and deeds that would try to derail him/her from Your purpose for his/her life. Because _____ pays attention to Your words, they will bring life and healing to his/her entire body.

Isaiah 54:17
Proverbs 4:22

HEARING GOD'S VOICE . . .

_____ hears God's voice because he/she knows Him and follows Him. He/She does not follow the voice of a stranger.

John 10:3-5,27

_____'s own ears will hear the voice of the Lord. His/Her relationship with the Lord is so intimate that right behind him/her _____ will hear His guiding voice that says, "This is the way you should go," whether to the right or to the left.

Isaiah 30:21

HELP . . .

The Lord is _____'s help so he/she does not need to fear what man may try to do to him/her. The Lord will strengthen _____ and help him/her.

He will hold him/her up during difficult times. When _____ goes through deep waters, God will be with him/her. When he/she goes through rivers of difficulty, he/she will not drown for God is always with him/her.

Hebrews 13:6
Isaiah 41:10-13
Isaiah 43:2

In times of trouble the Lord will hold _____'s head up high above the enemies that surround him/her. He will conceal him/her safely when trouble comes. When he/she calls on Your name in times of trouble, You will help him/her for Your name is a strong tower and _____ runs into it and is safe. You are his/her security and will keep him/her from being caught in any trap.

Psalm 27:5-6
Proverbs 18:10
Proverbs 3:26

HUMILITY . . .

_____ possesses an attitude of humility. He/She will not adopt a proud attitude toward us or others and so it will bring him/her honor, riches, and life. _____ clothes himself/herself with humility for God resists the proud but gives grace to the humble.

Proverbs 15:33 AMP
Proverbs 22:4
1 Peter 5:5

IDENTITY . . .

_____ is a new creation in Christ Jesus, born anew of the Spirit of God, and cleansed with the shed blood of Jesus Christ. He/She is a child of God, redeemed from the hand of the enemy. Christ's nature and His ability are within him/her so that he/she no longer fulfills the lust of the flesh.

2 Corinthians 5:17
1 John 1:7
Romans 8:16
Psalm 107:2

_____ is created in the likeness and image of God. In other words, he/she is cut out of His mold—created for good works as a servant of Jesus Christ and as a representative of Him in the earth. _____ is maturing in Him because he/she faithfully reads, studies, and meditates on His Word daily. No matter how busy his/her schedule becomes, _____ makes prayer and communion with the Lord an important part of each day.

Genesis 1:26
Ephesians 2:10
Joshua 1:8

_____ is more than a conqueror—a winner in everything he/she undertakes at God's direction through Christ who loves him/her.

Romans 8:37

INTEGRITY . . .

_____ lives a life of integrity and so is able to maneuver safely through life. Everything he/she does reflects integrity. His/Her life is an example of good works of every kind.

Proverbs 10:9

LIFE . . .

God has set before _____ life and death, blessing and cursing. Therefore, _____ chooses life and blessing!

Deuteronomy 30:19

LIFESTYLE . . .

_____'s body is the temple of the Holy Spirit who resides in him/her. He/She chooses to keep himself/herself pure before the Lord in his/her heart, mind, and body. _____ keeps himself/herself sexually pure until the day he/she marries. He/She also makes wise choices as to what he/she puts into his/her body. _____ chooses to eat healthy food and to escape the temptation of alcohol, drugs, and addictions so that he/she will glorify God in his/her body and in his/her spirit.

1 Corinthians 6:19-20

LOVE . . .

_____ is a child of God and loves God with all his/her heart, soul, mind, and strength. _____ chooses to love others with the same manner and measure of love with which God loves him/her. He/She is patient and kind, not boastful, jealous, proud, or rude. _____ does not demand his/her own way. He/She is not irritable. He/She keeps no record of the times he/she has been wronged. He/She does not rejoice about injustice, but he/she does rejoice when truth wins out. _____ never gives up and he/she never loses faith. He/She is always hopeful and will remain steadfast and strong through every circumstance. The love of God in _____ will last forever.

Deuteronomy 6:5
John 13:34-35
Matthew 22:37-40
1 Corinthians 13:4-8 NLT

_____ is kind to those who are cruel to him/her. He/She chooses to love his/her enemies and to do good to those who are hateful to him/her. He/She is quick to bless those who curse him/her and pray for those who try to bring him/her harm. He/She makes it his/her practice to treat others the way he/she would want to be treated. In doing so, his/her life is a shining example of God's love to the world.

Matthew 5:44
Matthew 7:12

A MERRY HEART . . .

_____ is a joyful child and has a merry heart which is like a medicine to his/her body. Joy bubbles forth from him/her and it affects the attitudes and actions of others in positive ways! He/She brings joy to his/her parents, his/her siblings, his/her teachers, and people enjoy being around him/her. In fact, joy is the source of his/her strength.

Proverbs 17:22
Nehemiah 8:10

MIGHTY . . .

_____ will be mighty upon the earth. As he/she grows up, moves out and establishes a home of his/her own, it will be filled with wealth and riches because of the provision God has already made for _____. His righteousness endures in _____ forever!

Psalm 112:2-3

MONEY MANAGEMENT . . .

_____ is a good manager (a wise steward) of his/her money. He/She is a tither and a generous giver. Because he/she seeks first the Kingdom of God, everything he/she needs will be provided at the right time. God is in first place in _____'s financial priorities. Because he/she honors God in this manner, the Lord is honoring _____!

Matthew 6:33
Malachi 3:8-12

MOTIVES . . .

Everything _____ does, he/she does heartily as unto the Lord and not unto men. He/She delights in doing the will of God and not seeking his/her own will or way. Instead, as he/she submits his/her heart to the Lord, He is guiding him/her down paths of peace.

Colossians 3:23

Jesus had the heart of a servant. Thank You, Lord, that You are creating that same heart in _____. Because _____ is modeling his/her life after You, Lord, his/her heart is to lift and serve others in ways that will cause them to want a relationship with You as well.

Matthew 20:26-28
Mark 9:35

NO CONDEMNATION . . .

Thank You that _____ is free from the condemnation that the world would try to put upon him/her. Jesus did not come to the world to condemn it, but to save it. As _____ receives Your salvation, he/she walks from condemnation of the sins of the past. Because he/she is living and walking in obedience to the Holy Spirit, he/she has a heart tender to His correction and will quickly turn back to Your path should he/she make a wrong choice. Each day he/she draws closer to You.

John 3:17
Romans 8:1

OBEDIENCE . . .

_____ is willing and obedient to those in authority starting with us as his/her parents. Because he/she is obedient, he/she will eat the good of the land. He/She is respectful to those in authority in the government arena—local, state, national, and international—and prays faithfully for officials in these areas.

Isaiah 1:19
Ephesians 6:1-3
1 Timothy 2:1-4

PATIENCE . . .

_____ is patient and full of self-control.

Galatians 5:22-23

PEACE . . .

_____ is taught of the Lord and great is his/her peace and undisturbed composure. God is talking to him/her today and he/she hears and obeys! The peace of God keeps _____'s heart and mind in perfect peace so that he/she can trust in Him. His peace in him/her produces a quietness and confidence that cannot be shaken.

Isaiah 54:13 AMP
Philippians 4:7
Isaiah 32:17

PRAISE . . .

_____ has a heart to worship You, Lord, and it is a part of his/her daily lifestyle. Each morning, _____ takes the time to enter into Your presence with praise for all You have done. He/She has a thankful heart and never forgets all that You have done in his/her life. His/Her faith is growing by leaps and bounds as he/she recounts the wondrous things You have done in his/her life and will continue to do as _____ continues to put You first.

Psalm 100
Psalm 126

PRAYER . . .

_____ remembers to devote himself/herself to prayer with an alert mind and a thankful heart. No matter how busy his/her schedule gets, he/she will set aside a designated time each day to pray. As he/she lifts his/her petitions to You, Lord, You hear his/her prayer and You said You would answer and show him/her things to come. I pray that _____ will learn to take time, after he/she prays, to listen for Your instruction and to hear Your voice.

Colossians 4:2
Jeremiah 33:3
1 Corinthians 14:13-15

PRIORITY #1 . . .

_____'s number one priority is to love the Lord God with all his/her heart, with all his/her soul, with all his/her strength, and with all his/her mind. He/She also makes it a point to love his/her neighbor as himself/herself as Your Word commands. As _____ seeks first God's Kingdom and His righteousness—His way of doing and being right—all the things he/she needs will be added to him/her.

Luke 10:27 AMP
Matthew 6:33 AMP

PROMOTION . . .

Promotion comes from the Lord. He puts down one and lifts up another. As _____ is obedient to You, Lord, You said that You would open doors for him/her that no one can shut, and You would close doors that no one can open. That the gift You have placed within _____ would open doors for him/her and bring him/her before great men. Father, I thank You that You desire to promote _____ because he/she is obedient to Your Word and he/she will never deny Your name in any situation.

Though _____'s beginning may be small and insignificant, his/her latter end will increase abundantly.

Psalm 75:6-7 AMP
Revelation 3:7-8
Proverbs 18:16
Job 8:7

PROPHECY ...

God is pouring out His Spirit upon _____. He is going to use him/her mightily for His glory and he/she will prophesy in His name and be an encouragement wherever he/she goes.

Acts 2:17

PROSPERITY ...

_____ magnifies the Lord, for He takes pleasure in his/her prosperity—spirit, soul, and body. God supplies all of his/her needs according to His riches in glory by Christ Jesus. God causes _____ to have peace and prosperity in every area of his/her life. His desire for him/her is that he/she will prosper in all things and be in health, just as his/her soul prospers. No good thing will He withhold from _____ because he/she walks uprightly!

Psalm 35:27
Philippians 4:19
Psalm 147:13

3 John 2
Psalm 84:11

PROTECTION . . .

No weapon formed against _____ will prosper. Part of his/her godly heritage is that _____ will be able to refute every word spoken against him/her in judgment, calling all of the words null and void that do not agree with what God says about him/her in His Word and by His Spirit.

Isaiah 54:17

The Lord is a shelter for _____, a strong tower from the enemy. He/She will abide in His tabernacle forever and trust in the shelter of God's wings. Because he/she listens to You, Lord, he/she will live in peace, untroubled by fear of harm.

Psalm 61:3-4
Proverbs 1:33

Greater is He who is in _____ than he who is in this world.

1 John 4:4

The Lord will cause the enemies who rise up against _____ to be defeated before his/her face. They may come out against him/her one way, but they will flee before him/her seven ways.

Deuteronomy 28:7

No evil will befall _____ and no plague shall come near his/her dwelling for God has given His angels charge over _____ to keep, defend, and preserve him/her in all of his/her ways all the days of his/her life.

Psalm 91:10-11

_____ is a child of God. Because of this, he/she has been given authority and power (physical and mental strength and ability) over all the power that the enemy possesses, and nothing shall in any way harm _____.

Luke 10:19 AMP

REDEEMED . . .

_____ is redeemed from the curse of the law and has received all of His blessings as an heir of Jesus Christ. He/She is redeemed with His precious blood. Because he/she has accepted Jesus as his/her Savior, He has given him/her wisdom, righteousness, sanctification, and redemption.

Galatians 3:13-14
1 Peter 1:18-19
Hebrews 9:12
1 Corinthians 1:30
Colossians 1:13-14

RENEWING YOUR MIND . . .

_____ has presented and surrendered his/her body as a living sacrifice to God. He/She is in a process of transformation by the renewal of his/her mind daily with God's Word. As this transformation takes place, he/she looks and acts more like Jesus each day!

Romans 12:1-2

REST ...

When _____ is weary or carrying a heavy burden, he/she will remember to come to You so that he/she will receive rest. When he/she runs the race of life, he/she will not grow weary and as he/she walks through each situation, he/she will not faint, for You are giving him/her a place of rest. Because he/she puts his/her trust in You, he/she will find new strength and will soar high above the situation at hand.

Matthew 11:28
Isaiah 40:30-31

SALVATION ASSURED ...

God will contend with those who contend with _____ and He will save him/her.

Isaiah 49:25

SCHOOL ...

Thank You, Lord, that _____ has a thirst for knowledge and applies himself/herself in his/her studies. He/She does not waste the skills and gifts you have given him/her but makes good use of his/her time developing his/her mind and talents. Help him/her to always use these gifts for Your glory. Give him/her godly teachers with hearts of understanding. Help him/her not to be led astray by false philosophies, but to remain steadfast in You.

Colossians 2:8
Isaiah 11:2

SLEEP . . .

When it is time to sleep, _____ is able to fall asleep quickly and peacefully. He/She has undisturbed sleep, free from fearful dreams. He/She goes to bed each night without fear and will lie down and sleep soundly. He/She is able to enter into rest and awakes with his/her strength renewed full of Your life and energy.

Psalm 3:5
Psalm 4:8
Joshua 1:13
Psalm 23
Proverbs 3:24-25

SOUNDNESS OF MIND . . .

God has not given _____ a spirit of fear, but of power, love, and a sound mind. His/Her thoughts and his/her ways are becoming like God's thoughts and ways. He/She is quick to cast down imaginations and everything that exalts itself above the knowledge of God.

_____ has an anointed mind, the mind of Christ. He/She is quick to learn because like Daniel, light and understanding and excellent wisdom are found within him/her.

2 Timothy 1:7
Isaiah 55:8-9
1 Corinthians 2:16
2 Corinthians 10:5
Daniel 5:14

STANDARD . . .

_____ chooses the Word of God to be the ultimate standard for his/her life, which is living and powerful, and sharper than any two-edged sword. As he/she studies the Bible and hides Your Word in his/her heart, it acts as his/her guide and is a discerner of the thoughts and intents of the heart.

Hebrews 4:12
Psalm 119:105

SUBMISSIVE . . .

_____ is obedient and submissive to those who are in authority over him/her. He/She does not rebel against authority, but understands that they must watch out for his/her soul and give an account of their care of him/her. _____ is a blessing to those who are over him/her in leadership and remembers to pray for them diligently so that they will make wise decisions.

Hebrews 13:17
1 Peter 2:18-21

TEMPTATION . . .

No matter what temptation comes across _____'s path today, he/she will be able to resist it and run from it. God is always faithful in that He will provide a way of escape for _____ from any temptation and _____ will choose that way of escape.

1 Corinthians 10:13

TRAINED . . .

_____ has been trained in the way he/she should go, and as he/she grows up he/she will not depart from this godly training. Instead, he/she lives a life that brings You glory and honor.

Proverbs 22:6 KJV

UNIQUELY CREATED . . .

_____ is fearfully and wonderfully created by our Creator God. He/She was woven together in the depths of the earth. God orchestrated the entire process, making him/her a unique individual. He/She was formed in His likeness and image. God created him/her for a specific purpose and He will fulfill His plan for him/her upon the earth. He/She is destined for greatness!

Psalm 139:13-18 NIV
Genesis 1:26-27

VALUE . . .

_____ is valuable to the Lord because of the price that was paid for him/her—Jesus' blood! He/She is a special treasure unto Him for he/she obeys His voice and keeps His covenant. God loves and values _____ so much, that He rejoices over him/her with gladness and with singing!

Exodus 19:5
Zephaniah 3:17

VICTORY . . .

God always leads _____ in triumph in Christ and spreads through him/her the knowledge of Jesus everywhere he/she goes. The Lord causes _____ to be a winner—a champion—in every realm of life! He/She is like salt and light in the earth and his/her light shines brightly so that others will see his/her good works and glorify the Father in heaven!

2 Corinthians 2:14
1 Corinthians 15:57
Matthew 5:13-16

VISIONS AND DREAMS . . .

God is pouring out His Spirit upon _____. He/She makes himself/herself available for the Lord to work through him/her. The Scripture says that in the last days that old men will dream dreams and young men will see visions. No matter whether _____ is young or even when he/she is old, the Lord will use him/her mightily.

Joel 2:28

WISDOM . . .

In Christ are hidden all the treasures of wisdom and knowledge. Because _____ is in Him, those treasures are within him/her. They will dominate his/her thinking and actions as he/she meditates in the Word and prays. He/She is increasing in wisdom and in stature and in favor with God and men just as Jesus did!

Colossians 2:3
Luke 2:52

_____ is a wise person and is hungry for knowledge. He/She receives instruction gladly. He/She has a reverential fear of the Lord, so he/she has wisdom and is developing good judgment.

Proverbs 15:14
Proverbs 10:8
Proverbs 4:7

WORDS . . .

The words _____ speaks are words of life, not death. He/She is wise with his/her words knowing that a soft, gentle answer turns away wrath, but a harsh word stirs up anger. When trapped by his/her own words, _____ is quick to humble himself/herself and repent. He/She is like a guardian over his/her own mouth because right words spoken at an appropriate time will save his/her soul from troubles.

Proverbs 18:20-21
Proverbs 15:1 NIV
Proverbs 6:2-3
Proverbs 15:23
Proverbs 21:23

_____ speaks kind words that are like honey. They are sweet to the soul and healthy for the body. His/Her speech is wise and his/her words are persuasive. He/She does not use foul or abusive language. Instead, everything he/she says is good and helpful and an encouragement to all who hear it. His/Her conversation is gracious and attractive so that he/she will have the right response for everyone.

Proverbs 16:23-24
Ephesians 4:29
Colossians 4:6

OTHER BOOKS BY
DR. BILLY JOE DAUGHERTY:

No Fear

Knocked Down But Not Out

God Is Not Your Problem

When Life Throws You a Curve

You Can Be Healed

101 Days of Absolute Victory

Living in God's Abundance

Led By the Spirit

Breaking the Chains of Bondage

Principles of Prayer

BOOKS BY SHARON DAUGHERTY

What Guys See that Girls Don't ... Or Do They?

Avoiding Deception

Known By Your Fruit

ABOUT THE AUTHOR

Dr. Billy Joe Daugherty

Dr. Billy Joe Daugherty is founder and pastor of Victory Christian Center in Tulsa, Oklahoma, with over 17,000 members. He is also the founder of Victory Christian School, Victory Bible Institute and Victory World Missions Training Center, which are raising up men and women to reach the nations for Jesus. More than 845 Victory Bible Institutes have been started in 91 countries around the world.

Victory Christian Center founded *The Tulsa Dream Center*, which provides food and clothing distribution, a dental/medical clinic, legal counseling, recreation facilities and other programs to help needy people of Tulsa. Victory Kidz Outreach ministry brings 1,200-1,600 children and teens in from this area each week for *Kidz Ministry* and *Chosen* Youth ministry.

His daily radio and television broadcast, "Victory in Jesus," reaches more than 75 million households in North America as well as multitudes internationally via satellite and the Internet. He is the author of many books, including *No Fear, 101 Days of Absolute Victory, Knocked Down But Not Out, God Is Not Your Problem,* and *This New Life.*

Billy Joe and his wife, Sharon, minister God's healing, saving, and delivering power as a team. Sharon's music, exhortation, and prophetic words release the anointing of the Holy Spirit to set people free. Billy Joe preaches and ministers the living Word of victory in Jesus. Signs and wonders follow their ministry.

Their four children and two sons-in-law work in ministry as well.

For more information visit
www.victory.com

www.victory.com

For the latest information in book news, author information and itinerary, please visit us on the Web at www.victory.com. Watch live services or sign up to receive our weekly full sermon audio podcast, take Victory on your mp3 player or listen on your computer, and more!

Additional copies of this book and other books from Dr. Billy Joe Daugherty are available at your local bookstore.

For more information about the ministry or to receive a product catalog, you may contact:

www.victory.com

or

Victory Christian Center
7700 South Lewis Avenue
Tulsa, OK 74136 U.S.A.
(918) 491-7700